흥부전

The Story of Heungbu

머리말

"다락원 한국어 학습문고" 시리즈는 대표적인 한국 문학 작품을 한국어 학습자들의 읽기 수준에 맞도록 재구성하여 쉽고 재미있게 독해력을 증진할 수 있도록 하였습니다. '국제 통용 한국어 표준 교육 과정'과 '한국어 교육 어휘 내용 개발'을 기준으로 초급부터 고급(A1~C2)으로 구분하여 지문을 읽으면서 각자의 수준에 맞는 필수 어휘와 표현을 자연스럽게 익힐 수 있습니다.

시대적 배경과 관련된 어휘에는 별도의 설명을 추가하여 그 당시 문화에 대해 이해하면서 본문을 읽을 수 있도록 하였습니다. 더불어 의미 전달에 충실한 번역문과 내용 이해 문제를 수록하여 자신의 이해 정도를 점검하고 확인할 수 있도록 하였고, 전문 성우가 직접 낭독한 음원을 통해 눈과 귀를 동시에 활용한 독해 연습이 가능하도록 하였습니다.

"다락원 한국어 학습문고" 시리즈를 통해 보다 유익하고 재미있는 한국어 학습이 되시길 바랍니다.

다락원 한국어 학습문고
저자 대표 **김유미**

Preface

The Darakwon Korean Readers series adapts the most well-known Korean literary works to the reading levels of Korean language learners, restructuring them into simple and fun stories that encourage the improvement of reading comprehension skills. Based on the "International Standard Curriculum for the Korean Language" and "Research on Korean Language Education Vocabulary Content Development", the texts have been graded from beginner to advanced levels (A1~C2) so that readers can naturally learn the necessary vocabulary and expressions that match their level.

With supplementary explanations concerning historical background, learners can understand the culture of the era as they read. In addition, students can assess and confirm their understanding with the included reading comprehension questions and translations faithful to the meaning of the original text. Recordings of the stories by professional voice actors also allow reading practice through the simultaneous use of learners' eyes and ears.

We hope that Darakwon Korean Readers series will provide learners with a more fruitful and interesting Korean language learning experience.

Darakwon Korean Readers
Kim Yu Mi, Lead Author

일러두기

How to Use This Book

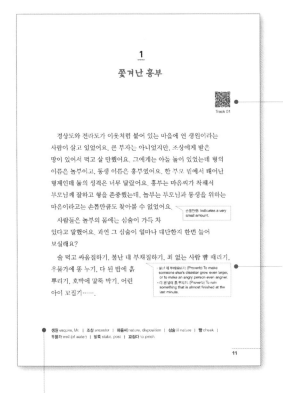

듣기 Listening

QR 코드를 통해 전문 성우가 녹음한 정확하고 생생한 작품 낭독을 들을 수 있습니다.

Using the corresponding QR codes, learners can access professional recordings of the story.

해설 Notes

학습자들이 내용을 이해하는 데 필요한 한국어 문법, 표현, 어휘, 속담, 문화적 배경 등을 알기 쉽게 설명해 주어 별도로 사전을 찾을 필요가 없도록 하였습니다.

Explanations on essential Korean grammar, expressions, vocabulary, proverbs, cultural background, etc. are provided to learners so aid understanding without the need to consult a separate dictionary.

어휘 설명 Vocabulary Explanation

각 권의 수준에 맞춰 본문에서 꼭 알아야 하는 필수 어휘를 영어 번역과 함께 제시하였습니다.

English translations are provided for the essential vocabulary matched to the level of each title.

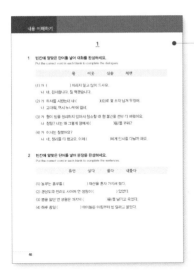

내용 이해하기 Reading Comprehension

다양한 문제를 통해 본문 내용 이해와 함께 해당 레벨에서 알아야 할 문형과 어휘를 다시 한번 확인할 수 있습니다.

Learners can check their understanding of the main text while also reviewing the essential sentence patterns and vocabulary for their level through various comprehension questions.

본문 번역 Text Translations

한국어 본문 내용을 정확히 이해할 수 있도록 의미 전달에 충실한 영어 번역을 수록하였습니다.

An English translation faithful to the original text is included to ensure an exact understanding of the original Korean story.

모범 답안 Answers

모범 답안과 비교하며 자신의 이해 정도를 스스로 평가하고 진단할 수 있습니다.

Learners can self-evaluate and assess their level of understanding by comparing their answers to the answer key.

작품 소개

흥부전

"흥부전"은 한국의 대표적인 고전 소설로 "춘향전", "심청전"과 더불어 한국 사람들이 가장 좋아하는 이야기입니다. 조선 시대에 지어진 한글 소설이며, 판소리계 소설로 지은이가 누구인지 언제 지어졌는지 알 수 없습니다. 판소리는 이야기 전체가 노래 가사 같다는 점에서 뮤지컬과 비슷하지만 여러 명이 공연하는 뮤지컬과 다르게 한 명의 소리꾼이 노래도 부르고 이야기도 한다는 특징이 있습니다. 또 관객들에게 웃음과 재미를 줄 수 있는 대사가 많이 있어서 해학과 풍자가 뛰어납니다.

"흥부전"의 배경이 된 조선 후기에는 상업이 발달하면서 부에 대한 인식이 달라졌습니다. 끼니를 걱정할 만큼 가난한 양반이 있는가 하면, 장사로 돈을 많이 벌어 부유해진 백성도 있었습니다. 그리고 당시에는 제사를 지내는 첫째 아들이 부모님의 재산을 모두 물려받는 것이 일반적이었습니다. "흥부전"은 이러한 시대적 배경을 바탕으로 부모님이 남긴 재산을 독차지한 욕심 많은 형 놀부와 가난하지만 착한 동생 흥부에 관한 이야기가 전개됩니다.

흥부는 당시에 가난하고 소외된 서민층을 대표하는 인물로, 서민들은 "흥부전"을 통해 놀부로 대표되는 나쁜 사람들을 욕하면서 스트레스를 해소하는 한편, 착하게 열심히 살다 보면 복을 받을 수 있다는 위로와 희망을 얻을 수 있었습니다. 그런데 요즘은 흥부를 현실 감각이 부족하고 무능력한 인물로, 놀부를 경제에 밝은 인물로 바라보기도 합니다. "흥부전"을 읽고 등장인물에 대한 여러분의 생각을 이야기해 봅시다.

Introduction to the Story

The Story of Heungbu

The classic Korean novel "The Story of Heungbu," along with "The Story of Chunhyang" and "The Story of Shimcheong," is one of Korea's most beloved stories. "The Story of Heungbu" is a novel written in Hangeul during the Joseon Dynasty. As a pansori novel, there is no way of knowing who wrote it or when it was written. Pansori is similar to a musical in the way that it tells an entire story through song lyrics, but unlike musicals, which are performed by multiple people, pansori has the unique trait of being sung by only one singer. In addition, there are many lines of dialogue to make the audience smile and laugh, so the humor and satire of pansori is outstanding.

"The Story of Heungbu" is set in the second half of the Joseon Dynasty, when people's understanding of wealth changed as commerce became more developed. There were people who were so poor that they worried about their meals, but there were also people who became wealthy by earning a lot of money through business. And in those days, it was common for the firstborn son, who performed the ancestral rites, to inherit all of his parents' assets. "The Story of Heungbu," which is set in this time period, is a story about a greedy older brother named Nolbu who takes all of his parents' assets for himself and his poor but kind younger brother Heungbu.

Heungbu is a character who represents the poor and marginalized working class of that time period. On one hand, ordinary people used "The Story of Heungbu" to relieve their stress as they cursed the evil people represented by Nolbu; on the other hand, they found comfort and hope in the idea that if a person was kind and works hard, they could receive good fortune like Heungbu. However, these days Heungbu is seen as an incompetent character who lacks a sense of reality, and Nolbu is seen as a character with a sharp sense of the economy. Read "The Story of Heungbu" and share your thoughts about the characters in the story.

목차
Table of Contents

머리말 Preface ………………………………………………………………… 2

일러두기 How to Use This Book …………………………………………… 4

작품 소개 Introduction to the Story …………………………………… 6

등장인물 Characters ……………………………………………………… 10

1 쫓겨난 흥부 Heungbu is Cast Out ………………………………… 11

2 놀부에게 도움을 거절당한 흥부 Nolbu Refuses to Help Heungbu …… 16

3 매를 맞아 돈을 벌려는 흥부 Heungbu Tries to Earn Money by Being Beaten …… 21

4 제비를 구해 준 흥부 Heungbu Saves a Swallow ………………… 26

5 박 자르는 흥부네 Heungbu's Family Cuts Open the Gourds …… 29

6 흥부 집을 방문한 놀부 Nolbu Visits Heungbu's House ………… 33

7 제비 잡으러 나가는 놀부 Nolbu Goes to Catch a Swallow …… 37

8 박 자르는 놀부네 Nolbu's Family Cuts Open the Gourds ……… 40

9 사이좋은 형제 Close Brothers ……………………………………… 45

부록 Appendix

내용 이해하기 Reading Comprehension ………………………………… 48

모범 답안 Answers ……………………………………………………… 68

본문 번역 Text Translations …………………………………………… 70

흥부전

The Story of Heungbu

등장인물
Characters

흥부
Heungbu

마음씨 착하고 인정이 많다.
못된 형을 미워하지 않는다.

A kind and tender-hearted
man. He does not hate his
wicked brother.

흥부 아내
Heungbu's Wife

흥부의 아내.
흥부처럼 착하고 정이 많다.

Heungbu's wife. Like
Heungbu, she is kind and
warm-hearted.

놀부
Nolbu

흥부의 형. 아버지의 재산을
혼자 차지하고 흥부를
내쫓는다.

Heungbu's older brother.
He takes all of their father's
wealth for himself and
drives Heungbu away.

놀부 아내
Nolbu's Wife

놀부의 아내. 놀부처럼
욕심이 많고 인정이 없다.

Nolbu's wife. Like Nolbu,
she is greedy and cold-
hearted.

제비
The Swallow

흥부 덕분에 목숨을 건지고,
그 은혜를 갚기 위해 돌아온다.

Thanks to Heungbu, the
swallow escapes death. It
returns to repay Heungbu's
kindness.

구렁이
The Serpent

옛날이야기에서 무섭거나
신기한 힘을 가진 동물로 자주
나온다. 제비를 잡아먹으려다
실패한다.

In old stories, serpents
often appear as frightening
creatures with amazing
powers. The serpent tries to
catch and eat the swallow,
but fails.

1

쫓겨난 흥부

Track 01

경상도와 전라도가 이웃처럼 붙어 있는 마을에 연 생원이라는
사람이 살고 있었어요. 큰 부자는 아니었지만, 조상에게 받은
땅이 있어서 먹고 살 만했어요. 그에게는 아들 둘이 있었는데 형의
이름은 놀부이고, 동생 이름은 흥부였어요. 한 부모 밑에서 태어난
형제인데 둘의 성격은 너무 달랐어요. 흥부는 마음씨가 착해서
부모님께 잘하고 형을 존중했는데, 놀부는 부모님과 동생을 위하는
마음이라고는 손톱만큼도 찾아볼 수 없었어요.

> 손톱만큼: Indicates a very
> small amount.

사람들은 놀부의 몸에는 심술이 가득 차
있다고 말했어요. 과연 그 심술이 얼마나 대단한지 한번 들어
보실래요?

술 먹고 싸움질하기, 불난 데 부채질하기, 죄 없는 사람 뺨 때리기,
우물가에 똥 누기, 다 된 밥에 흙
뿌리기, 호박에 말뚝 박기, 어린
아이 꼬집기……

> • 불난 데 부채질하기: (Proverb) To make
>   someone else's disaster grow even larger,
>   or to make an angry person even angrier.
> • 다 된 밥에 흙 뿌리기: (Proverb) To ruin
>   something that is almost finished at the
>   last minute.

생원 esquire, Mr. | **조상** ancestor | **마음씨** nature, disposition | **심술** ill nature | **뺨** cheek |
우물가 well (of water) | **말뚝** stake, post | **꼬집다** to pinch

형과 달리 동생 흥부는 온 동네 사람들이 칭찬할 정도였어요. 동네 어른에게 인사하기, 이웃과 사이좋게 지내기, 굶는 사람에게 밥 덜어 주기, 추위에 떠는 사람에게 자기 옷 벗어 주기, 길 잃은 아이 부모 찾아 주기……

흥부는 길거리에 있는 돌멩이조차 함부로 차지 않는 착한 사람이었어요. 놀부는 이런 흥부를 볼 때마다 눈엣가시 같았어요.

그러던 어느 날 오랫동안 병을 앓던 연 생원이 다음과 같은 유언을 남기고 세상을 떠났어요.

> 눈엣가시: Used when talking about a person that the subject hates so much that they hate seeing them.

"얘들아, 아무래도 내가 오래 살지 못할 것 같구나. 저 양지 쪽에 있는 땅은 흥부네 몫이고 나머지는 놀부네가 모두 가지거라. 대신 동생을 잘 돌봐야 한다. 내가 죽어도 지금처럼 이 집에서 다 함께 행복하고 사이좋게 살도록 해라."

하지만 놀부는 아버지의 유언을 지킬 마음이 전혀 없었어요. 놀부는 흥부를 내쫓고 부모가 남긴 많은 재산을 혼자 가지려고 했어요.

덜다 to lessen | 돌멩이 stone | 병을 앓다 to suffer from a disease | 유언 will, testament |
세상을 떠나다 to pass away | 양지 sunny spot | 몫 share, portion | 내쫓다 to drive out, to kick out |
재산 assets, property

어느 날 놀부는 잠자는 흥부를 깨워 소리쳤어요.

"흥부야. 돈 벌 생각은 하지 않고 매일같이 놀고먹으니 보기 싫어 함께 못 살겠다. 비록 부모님이 남기신 재산이 있지만, 그건 마땅히 장손인 나의 몫이니, 너에게는 지푸라기 하나 줄 수 없다. 어려서는 형제가 같이 살아도 결혼하고 아이를 낳으면 각각 따로 사는 법이다. 그러니 지금 당장 네 식구들을 데리고 멀리 떠나거라."

> **TIP!** In the second half of the Joseon Dynasty, most parents left all of their assets to the eldest son.

흥부는 갑자기 무슨 말인지 몰라 가만히 듣고 있었어요.

"네가 나만 믿는 모양인데, 이제 더는 네 식구들을 먹이고 입히며 살 수 없다. 그러니 당장 내 집에서 나가 혼자 힘으로 살아 봐라. 돌아가신 아버지도 아마 내 생각과 같을 것이다."

> V + -는 모양이다: Used when looking at a different fact or situation and making a guess about what is happening or about a particular condition.

흥부는 하늘이 무너지는 듯했어요. 돌아가신 아버지가 무슨 일이 있어도 같이 살아가라고 했는데 형님이 갑자기 집을 나가라고 하니 앞으로 어떻게 해야 할지 알 수 없었어요.

> 하늘이 무너지다: (Figure of speech) Used when something very difficult and exhausting happens.

흥부는 땅바닥에 엎드려 놀부에게 사정했어요.

"아니, 형님. 갑자기 아내와 어린 자식들을 데리고 나가 어딜 가서 뭘 먹고 지낼 수 있겠습니까? 제발 그런 말씀 마세요."

놀고먹다 to live idly | **마땅히** rightfully, justly | **지푸라기** straw, hay | **법** a fixed reason or a duty that must be done | **당장** right away, immediately | **땅바닥** ground | **엎드리다** to lie down, to prostrate oneself | **사정하다** to beg | **제발** please, for heaven's sake

놀부가 화를 내며 소리쳤어요.

"지금까지 먹여 주고 입혀 주었더니 고마운 줄도 모르느냐?
장가를 들어 처자식을 두었으면 당연히 나가 살아야지. 당장 내
눈앞에서 사라져라!"

흥부는 울고불고 사정했지만, 놀부는 들은 척도 하지 않았어요.
흥부는 하는 수 없이 아내와 어린 자식들을
데리고 빈손으로 집을 나섰어요.

> V + -(으)ㄴ 척하다: Indicates
> the false appearance of a
> certain behavior or condition,
> but it is not actually real.

"아이고, 여보. 이렇게 갑자기 어디로 간단 말입니까?"

장가 marriage | 처자식 one's wife and children | 울고불고 to cry and scream | 빈손 empty hands

　불쌍한 흥부 아내는 어린 자식을 안고 업고 울면서 따라갔어요.
그러나 아무리 배가 고파도 먹을 게 없고, 밤이 깊어도 잘 데가
없었어요.

　하루 종일 쫄쫄 굶고 나니 아이들은 아침부터 밥 달라고 울기
시작했어요. 흥부는 이제 체면이고 뭐고 없었어요. 우선 집을 먼저
찾고 무슨 일이든 해야겠다고 생각했어요.

쫄쫄 starving ｜ **굶다** to go hungry ｜ **체면** face, honor

2

놀부에게 도움을 거절당한 흥부

Track 02

흥부는 그날부터 살 만한 곳을 계속 찾아다녔어요. 그러다 마침내 고향 근처 마을에서 쓰러져 가는 빈집을 발견했어요. 흥부는 간신히 그 집을 고쳐서 온 식구가 살 곳을 마련했어요. 비바람은 피할 수 있었지만 먹고 살 방법이 없었어요. 무슨 일이든지 가리지 않고 했지만 겨우 끼니를 거르지 않는 정도였어요.

> 끼니를 거르다: to miss a meal. 끼 is the appearance of food, so it means that a person went hungry and didn't eat a meal.

흥부 아내도 흥부를 도와 쉬지 않고 일했지만 사는 것이 너무 힘들고 어려웠어요. 이들은 가난했지만, 자식만큼은 부자였어요. 부부 사이가 좋아 일 년에 꼭 한 번씩은 자식을 낳았더니 자식들이 모두 스물아홉이었어요.

> V + -더니: Used when speaking about a certain result that came about after observing something in the past and learning a certain fact.

"엄마, 배고파요."

"엄마, 밥 주세요."

이 많은 자식들이 눈만 뜨면 밥 달라, 젖 달라 울거나 짜증을 냈어요. 흥부 아내는 서럽게 울다가 흥부를 보고 말했어요.

쓰러지다 to fall down, to collapse | 발견하다 to discover | 간신히 barely | 마련하다 to prepare, to arrange | 가리다 to distinguish, to be picky (about something) | 가난하다 to be poor | 젖 breast milk | 서럽다 to be sorrowful

"여보, 제발 잘사는 형님 댁에 가서 쌀 좀 얻어 오세요. 우리는 굶어 죽을지라도 불쌍한 내 새끼들은 살려야 되지 않겠어요."

"형님 댁에 가는 것은 어렵지 않지만, 가도 쌀을 내주겠소?"

"주시고 안 주시고는 나중 문제고 우선은 한번 찾아 가 보세요. 이대로는 내 새끼들 다 굶어 죽겠어요."

흥부는 차마 발길이 떨어지지 않았지만, 쌀을 담을 자루 하나 메고 집을 나왔어요. 드디어 놀부 집에 도착해 '흠흠' 기침을 하며 안으로 들어갔어요. 하인인 마당쇠가 흥부를 막아섰지만 바로 흥부를 알아보고 인사했어요.

> 발길이 떨어지지 않다: Means the subject does not want to leave or is reluctant to leave.

"아이고, 작은 서방님이시군요. 제가 서방님 얼굴도 알아보지 못했습니다."

> TIP! 하인 is a servant who works in someone else's home. In the past, servants who tended to the yard and ran small errands were called 마당쇠.

마당쇠는 흥부의 모습을 보고 눈물을 닦았어요. 말을 하지 않아도 흥부가 얼마나 고생을 했는지 한눈에 알 수 있었어요.

> TIP! In the past, commoners called young scholars, who did not have a government position, 서방님.

새끼 a condescending name for one's children | 내주다 to give | 차마 hardly able to bear doing something due to embarrassment or shame | 자루 sack | 메다 to carry over one's shoulder | 막아서다 to block, to fend off | 고생 hardship, suffering | 한눈에 at a glance

"형님은 방에 계시냐?"

마당쇠는 흥부를 방까지 데려다주고 얼른 뒤돌아섰어요.

"작은 서방님, 제가 모시고 왔다는 말은 하지 마세요."

흥부는 방을 향해 말했어요.

"형님, 형님, 흥부 왔습니다."

처음에는 아무 대답이 없어 흥부가 한 번 더 형님을 부르자 문이 열렸어요. 그렇지만 놀부는 처음 보는 사람을 대하듯 흥부를 모른 척했어요.

"누구신지요?"

"접니다, 흥부. 제가 형님 떠나 살다 보니 이 모양이 되었습니다. 하나밖에 없는 동생을 불쌍히 여기시고, 저 좀 도와주십시오."

흥부는 바닥에 주저앉아 엉엉 울며 말하였어요.

"뭘 잘못 알고 온 것 같은데 나는 외아들이고 동생은커녕 피붙이 하나 없습니다."

> • N + -은/는커녕: Indicates the negation of not only one thing but also something else on an even more telling, or serious level.
> • 피붙이: Refers to blood relatives such as parents, children, or siblings.

"형님, 제가 자주 인사 못 드려 화가 나신 모양인데 제가 이렇게 빌겠습니다. 아내와 어린 자식들이 굶어 죽게 생겼으니 먹을 것이라도 조금만 나누어 주십시오, 형님."

그 말이 끝나기가 무섭게 놀부의 담뱃대가 흥부에게 날아왔어요. 흥부는 깜짝 놀라 뒤로 넘어졌어요.

데려다주다 to bring someone somewhere | 뒤돌아서다 to turn around | 여기다 to regard, to consider | 주저앉다 to sink, to flop down | 엉엉 blubbering, bawling | 외아들 only son | 빌다 to beg (for something) | 담뱃대 tobacco pipe

"이놈아, 내가 너 주려고 쌀을 쌓아 둔 것도 아니고, 너 주려고
돈을 모은 것도 아니다.

옷이라도 줬으면 좋겠지만,

내가 입은 옷이 전부라 벗어 줄 수 없다. 그러니 딴 데 가서
알아봐라."

> 놈: Used when speaking with someone very familiar,
> or to speak condescendingly to another person.

"형님, 제발 식은 밥이라도 주십시오."

흥부가 나가지 않자, 놀부는 매를 들고 흥부를 사정없이 때렸어요.
옆에서 지켜보던 마당쇠는 발을 동동 구르며 걱정만 할 뿐 말릴 수
없었어요. 놀부를 말렸다가는 자기도 쫓겨날 게 뻔했어요.

흥부는 매를 피해 도망치다가
급한 마음에 부엌으로 들어갔어요.

> • 동동: (mimetic word) Used when describing
> that someone keeps lightly stamping their
> feet because they feel bad.
> • V + -(으)ㄹ 뻔하다: Used when the event in
> the preceding clause did not happen, but
> it very nearly happened.

그때 마침 놀부 아내는 주걱으로
밥을 푸고 있었어요. 며칠을 굶은 흥부는 구수한 밥 냄새를 맡자
아픈 것도 잊어버리고 형수님 옆으로 갔어요.

"형수님, 이 시동생에게 밥 한 그릇만 주십시오."

매 rod | 사정없이 mercilessly | 말리다 to stop someone from doing something | 도망치다 to escape,
to flee | 주걱 rice paddle | 푸다 to scoop out | 구수하다 to be savory | 형수 sister-in-law |
시동생 younger brother-in-law

그러자 바로 밥주걱이 흥부의 뺨으로 날아왔어요. 어찌나 세게
맞았는지 흥부는 볼에 불이 붙은 것처럼 화끈거렸어요. 손을 슬쩍
뺨에 대 보니 밥풀이 붙어 있어 그것을 얼른 입으로 집어넣었어요.
흥부는 형수님에게 밥풀이 많이 붙은 주걱으로 다른 쪽 뺨도 때려
달라고 하였어요. 놀부 아내는 그 말을 듣자마자 주걱을 내려놓고
부엌에서 불을 붙일 때 쓰는 부지깽이로

> V + –자마자: Used when the following clause happens immediately after the condition or situation in the preceding clause.

흥부를 실컷 때렸어요. 흥부는 차마
아프다는 말도 못 하고 아픈 몸을 질질
끌고 간신히 놀부 집에서 도망쳐 나왔어요.

어찌나 so, awfully | 볼 cheek | 화끈거리다 to burn, to flush | 밥풀 grain of steamed rice |
집어넣다 to put (in) | 부지깽이 poker (for fire) | 실컷 to one's heart's content | 질질 drag

3
매를 맞아 돈을 벌려는 흥부

Track 03

먹을 것을 얻으러 간 흥부가 늦도록 돌아오지 않자 흥부 아내는 걱정이 되었어요. 마을 밖까지 마중 나와 있는데 흥부가 마치 술에 취한 듯 비틀비틀 걸어왔어요. 흥부 아내는 반가운 마음에 달려가 흥부를 맞이했어요. 멀리서 살펴보니 흥부의 몸 어디에도 먹을 것은 보이지 않았어요. 그런데 가까이 가서 보니 남편의 이마에는 피가 나고 눈과 뺨은 잔뜩 부어 있었어요. 흥부 아내는 그런 남편의 모습을 보고 깜짝 놀라서 물었어요.

"아니, 얼굴은 왜 이래요? 혹시 형님에게 맞았어요?"

흥부는 아무리 자신을 서운하게 대한 형님이라도 차마 나쁘게 말할 수 없었어요.

"내가 형님께 쌀과 보리를 얻어 산길을 넘어오는데 세상에 못된 도둑을 만난 거요. 그 도둑들에게 곡식을 빼앗기고 형님이 주신 돈만은 뺏기지 않으려고 싸우다가 이렇게 되었소."

술에 취하다 to be drunk (on alcohol) | **비틀비틀** stagger | **맞이하다** to welcome, to greet | **잔뜩** very, extremely | **붓다** to swell | **서운하다** to hurt (feelings), to be sad | **보리** barley | **산길** mountain road | **도둑** thief | **빼앗기다** to be stolen

흥부 아내는 그 말이 거짓이라는 것을 알고 땅바닥에 주저앉아 엉엉 울었어요. 평소 놀부 형님의 성격을 봤을 때 무슨 일이 일어났는지 충분히 알 수 있었어요. 그렇게 당하고도 형님에 대해 좋게 말하려는 착한 흥부를 보며 더 마음이 아팠어요.

흥부는 아내를 달래 주고 아내는 흥부를 위로해 주었어요. 이 일을 겪고 난 후 흥부 아내는 무슨 일이든 들어오는 대로 다 했어요.

쿵덕쿵덕 곡식 찧기, 새벽에 물 떠 오기, 남의 집 잔치 음식 만들기, 남의 집 제사에서 설거지하기…….

> V + -는 대로: Indicates when a certain action or situation occurs, the following clause happens right then or immediately afterward.

흥부 아내처럼 흥부도 열심히 일했어요.

남의 집 똥 푸기, 한겨울에 농사 짓기, 동네 지붕 고치기 등 온갖 힘든 일은 다 했어요. 그러나 아무리 열심히 일해도 온 가족이 먹고 살기는 힘들었어요.

> **TIP!** 동네 지붕 고치기: This is the custom of repairing the roof of a thatched-roof house in late autumn to prepare for the cold winter.

하루는 흥부가 아내 몰래 곡식을 빌리려고 관청을 찾아갔어요. 그러나 땅도 없는 사람에게는 빌려줄 수 없다고 하자 흥부는 크게 실망하며 나왔어요. 그때 관청 직원이 조심스럽게 말했어요.

"혹시 매 맞아 본 적 있나?"

거짓 lie | 당하다 to suffer | 달래다 to soothe | 위로하다 to comfort | 쿵덕쿵덕 thumping noise | 곡식을 찧다 to thresh grain | 뜨다 to scoop up | 한겨울 in the middle of winter | 관청 government office | 조심스럽다 to be careful

그 직원은 옆 마을 부자 김 영감이 죄를 짓고 그 벌로 매 삼십 대를 맞아야 하는데 지금 병이 나서 누구를 대신 보내려고 한다고 말했어요.

> **TIP!** In the past, when someone committed a relatively minor crime, the person was punished by being spanked.

대신 매를 맞고 오면 돈 삼십 냥을 준다는 말에 흥부는 하겠다고 했어요. 자신만 눈 딱 감으면 온 식구가 배불리 먹을 수 있다고 생각했기 때문이에요. 관청 직원은 돈 다섯 냥을 먼저 주고 내일 아침에 관청으로 오라고 했어요.

> 눈 딱 감으면: Means that the subject is not thinking about anything else anymore. It is usually used in the form 눈 딱 감고.

흥부는 집 문 앞에서 큰 소리로 아내를 불렀어요. 흥부는 아내의 손 위에 다섯 냥을 올려놓으며 사실대로 말했어요. 흥부 아내는 남편이 매를 맞아 돈을 벌겠다는 말을 듣고 울기 시작했어요.

"당신이 매 맞고 벌어 온 돈으로 어떻게 쌀을 사서 먹을 수 있겠어요? 만약 당신이 매를 맞다 죽기라도 하면 나는 어린 자식 데리고 어떻게 살아요? 제발 그 돈 돌려주고 없었던 일로 하세요."

영감 elderly man | **냥** nyang, a unit for counting coins in olden times | **당신** you (pronoun)

흥부는 우는 아내를 안심시키고 다음 날 일찍 관청으로
달려갔어요.

"나는 김 영감 대신 매 맞으러 온 흥부라는 사람이오."

관청 직원 하나가 와서 흥부를 매 맞는 장소로 데리고 갔어요.

흥부는 엎드려 맞을 준비를 하고 있는데 어떤 사람이 와서 큰
소리로 말했어요.

"나라에 좋은 일이 생겨 사람을 죽인 경우 말고는 모두 풀어
주라는 소식이오. 그러니 어서 집으로 돌아가시오."

아니, 마른 하늘에 웬 날벼락인가요?

> 마른 하늘에 날벼락: (Proverb)
> Indicates an unexpected disaster
> in an unexpected situation.

흥부는 빈손으로 돌아가야 하는 자기
상황이 불쌍해서 눈물을 흘렸어요.
산길을 걸어 집으로 가는데 흥부 아내가 달려 나왔어요. 남편이 매
맞으러 간 사실을 알고 새벽에 우물에서 물을 떠 놓고 무사히 돌아와
달라고 빌고 있었어요. 무사히 돌아온 흥부를 보고 아내는 기쁨을
감추지 못했어요. 그런 아내를 보자
흥부는 더 마음이 아팠어요.

> TIP! In the past, people went to the
> well early in the morning to draw
> water and pray to their ancestors for
> the well-being of their families. This
> water is called "Jeonghwasu."

다음 날 김 영감의 아들이 찾아와 비록
매는 맞지 않았지만, 그 마음이 고맙다며 돈을 주고 갔어요. 흥부는
그 돈을 받지 않으려 했지만 몰래 돈을 두고 떠나 돌려줄 수도
없었어요. 활짝 웃는 아내를 보며 흥부도 오랜만에 기쁘게 웃었어요.

안심시키다 to reassure | 경우 case, scenario | 풀어 주다 to set free | 무사히 safely | 감추다 to hide,
to conceal | 비록 even though | 활짝 wide, broadly

4
제비를 구해 준 흥부

Track 04

날은 점점 따뜻해지고 삼월이 되었어요. 강남 갔던 제비들이
돌아와 흥부네 처마 밑에 집을 짓기 시작했어요.
아이들은 제비를 보고 기뻐했지만, 흥부는
튼튼하지 못한 곳에 제비 집을 짓는 제비 부부가
불쌍하다는 생각이 들었어요. 그러는 동안 제비

> 강남 간다: Used to describe swallows that fly south to a warmer place during the cold wintertime. 강남 is the region south of the Yangtze River in China.

부부는 뚝딱 집 한 채를 만들고 그 속에 알을 낳았어요. 얼마 후
알에서 예쁜 새끼 제비들이 나왔어요. 제비 부부는 열심히 먹이를
물어 날랐고 새끼 제비들은 먹이를 받아먹느라고 바빴어요.

그러던 어느 날 제비 부부가 집을
비운 사이 큰 구렁이 한 마리가 제비

> V + -느라고: Used when the action in the preceding clause is the reason or cause for the action in the following clause.

집으로 올라갔어요. 그것을 본 아이가 깜짝 놀라 소리쳤어요. 흥부가
나무 막대기를 들고 달려왔지만, 새끼 제비들은 모두 구렁이의
밥이 되고 한 마리밖에 남지 않았어요.

뚝딱 quickly, in a flash | 채 counting noun used for houses | 먹이 food | 물다 to hold in one's
mouth | 나르다 to carry, to transport | 받아먹다 to be fed | 비우다 to empty, to vacate |
막대기 stick

구렁이가 나머지 한 마리를 잡아먹으려 하는 순간, 놀란 새끼 제비가 포르르 날아오르다가 그만 땅에 떨어지고 말았어요.

흥부가 새끼 제비를 감싸 안고 자세히 살펴보니 오른쪽 다리가 부러져 있었어요.

"여보, 제비 다리가 부러졌소. 부러진 다리를 어서 치료해야겠소."

흥부는 새끼 제비를 정성을 다해 보살펴 주었어요. 새끼 제비는 조금씩 나아지더니 일주일이 지나자 날기 시작했어요. 제비 부부는 새끼에게 먹이 잡는 방법도 가르치고 하늘을 나는 방법도 가르쳤어요. 그러는 동안 여름이 가고 가을이 돌아왔어요.

"이제 너희들도 따뜻한 남쪽으로 떠날 때가 되었구나. 먼 길 잘 가거라. 우리 집 처마 밑을 비워 둘 테니 내년 봄에 꼭 다시 돌아오너라."

> V + -(으)ㄹ 테니: Indicates that the preceding clause includes the speaker's will, and becomes a condition for the following clause.

제비 가족은 흥부네 집을 떠나 따뜻한 제비 나라로 돌아왔어요. 제비 나라 임금님은 다리를 다친 제비를 발견하고 무슨 일인지 물었어요. 새끼 제비는 흥부네 집에서 있었던 일을 자세히 설명했어요.

"제비 목숨을 귀하게 여겨 보살펴 준 정성을 보답해야 할 텐데 어떻게 은혜를 갚는 게 좋을까?"

잡아먹다 to prey on | 감싸다 to cover up, to wrap up | 자세하다 to be detailed | 부러지다 to break, to fracture | 정성 sincerity, devotion | 보살피다 to look after | 임금님 ruler, monarch | 목숨 life | 귀하다 to be precious, to be valuable | 은혜를 갚다 to repay one's kindness

"예, 흥부를 가난에서 벗어나서 편히 살 수 있도록 해 주십시오."

제비 나라 임금님은 작은 박씨 하나를 제비에게 주었어요. 제비는 흥부에게 빨리 박씨를 전해 주고 싶어서 봄이 오기만을 기다렸어요.

드디어 봄이 왔어요. 제비는 박씨를 입에 물고 먼 길을 날아 흥부네 집에 도착했어요. 마당을 쓸고 있던 흥부가 제비를 알아보고 놀라 소리쳤어요.

"제비가 돌아왔다. 다리 다친 그 제비가 돌아왔어."

흥부는 집 나간 자식이 돌아온 것처럼 기뻐서 덩실덩실 춤을 추었어요. 제비는 그런 흥부 앞에 물고 온 박씨를 떨어뜨렸어요. 제비가 떨어뜨린 박씨를 받은 흥부는 그 박씨를 지붕 아래에 심었어요.

박씨 gourd seed | 쓸다 to sweep | 덩실덩실 lively, joyfully | 떨어뜨리다 to drop (something)

5

박 자르는 흥부네

Track 05

박씨를 심은 지 하루 만에 보름달 같은 박 네 개가 흥부네 지붕 위에 열렸어요. 크기도 얼마나 큰 지 지나가던 마을 사람들도 흥부네 박을 보며 놀랐어요.

어느덧 추석이 가까워졌어요. 다른 집에서는 음식 냄새가 코를 찌르는데 흥부네는 죽 한 그릇 끓일 쌀도 없었어요.

> 코를 찌르다: Indicates a strong smell being given off.

박을 잘라서 국을 끓여 먹기로 하고 온 식구가 마당에 모였어요. 흥부와 흥부의 아내는 마주 앉아 톱질을 하기 시작했어요.

"슬근슬근 톱질하세, 어서어서 톱질하세."

흥부가 밀면 흥부 아내는 당기고 그렇게 함께 외치면서 박을 자르니 재미도 있고 힘도 났어요.

> 슬근슬근: (mimetic word) Used when describing an action performed lightly or stealthily, without using much strength.

갑자기 박이 쩍 하고 갈라지더니 박 속에서 사내아이가 나왔어요. 그 아이는 화려한 병과 약초를 가득 내밀며 말했어요.

보름달 full moon | **열리다** to open | **어느덧** in no time, before one knows it | **추석** Chuseok (Korean Thanksgiving) | **마주** face to face | **톱질** sawing | **당기다** to pull | **갈라지다** to split, to crack | **약초** medicinal herb

"이것은 죽은 사람을 살리는 약이고 이것은 늙지 않는 약입니다. 여기에 수백 가지 만병통치약과 그 사용법이 있으니 잘 쓰세요."

말을 마치자 사내아이는 사라져 버렸어요.

> 만병통치약: A prescription or medicine used to cure any and all diseases.

흥부와 흥부 아내는 귀신에 홀린 듯 정신이 하나도 없었어요. 옆에 있던 아이들이 두 번째 박을 자르자고 고집부리는 바람에 흥부 부부는 다시 박을 자르기 시작하였어요.

> V + -는 바람에: Used when the action or condition in the preceding clause is the cause or reason for the following clause.

'펑!'

두 번째 박 속에서는 화려한 보물들이 쏟아져 나왔어요. 그리고 나무로 만든 두 개의 상자가 있었어요. 흥부가 궁금해서 살짝 열어 보니 하나는 쌀이 가득하고 하나는 돈이 가득했어요.

흥부와 아내는 기뻐하며 그 쌀로 큰 가마솥에다 밥을 짓고 그 돈으로 고기를 사다가 국을 끓여서는 잔뜩 먹었어요. 어찌나 배부른지 배가 터질 것 같았어요.

> 배가 터지다: Used when exaggerating being extremely full.

밥을 먹고 나서 흥부의 아들이 쌀이 들어 있는 상자를 열어 보고는 깜짝 놀랐어요. 상자에는 다시 쌀이 가득 들어 있었어요. 흥부가 돈이 들어 있는 상자를 열어 보니 그 안에도 돈이 가득했어요. 쌀과 돈을 자꾸 꺼내도 자꾸 다시 나왔어요.

사용법 directions | **사라지다** to disappear | **귀신에 홀리다** to be possessed by a ghost | **고집부리다** to insist, to be stubborn | **쏟아지다** to pour, to gush | **살짝** slightly | **가득하다** to be full | **가마솥** iron pot | **배부르다** to be full

"아버지, 이번에는 멋진 집이 갖고 싶어요.

아이들의 말에 흥부는 또다시 박을 자르기 시작했어요.

아이들의 소원대로 세 번째 박 속에서는 수십 명의 사람들이 나와 집을 짓기 시작했어요. 눈 깜짝할 사이에 커다란 집 한 채가 뚝딱 생겨났어요. 넓은 정원에 곡식이며 말이며 소며 모두 있었어요.

> 눈 깜짝할 사이: Indicates an extremely short period of time.

놀라서 입이 딱 벌어진 아내에게 흥부가 기쁜 목소리로 말했어요.

"여보, 우리 남은 박도 잘라 봅시다."

> 입이 딱 벌어지다: Used when someone is extremely surprised or dumbfounded.

마지막 박에서 나온 사람들은 집안일을 하기 시작했어요. 밤낮으로 남의 일을 해 주며 살아온 흥부네 식구들은 어쩔 줄 몰라 방으로 들어갔어요. 방에는 밥상 가득 많은 음식이 차려져 있었고, 비단옷에 이불까지 준비되어 있었어요.

"당신이 착하게 산 덕분에 우리가 이렇게 복을 받나 봐요."

아내의 말을 듣고 흥부는 그동안 함께 고생한 아내의 손을 잡아 주었어요.

그날부터 흥부네 가족은 좋은 집에서 비단옷을 입고 배부르게 먹으며 힘든 일은 할 필요 없이 행복하게 잘 살았어요.

소원 wish | 커다랗다 to be huge | 밤낮 day and night | 어쩔 줄 모르다 to not know what to do |
밥상 dining table | 차리다 to set, to prepare | 비단옷 silk clothes | 복 good fortune

6
흥부 집을 방문한 놀부

Track 06

흥부가 부자가 되었다는 소문은 바람을 타고 놀부의 귀에까지 들어갔어요.

"일해 주는 사람이 백 명이 넘고 창고에는 곡식이 꽉꽉 차고 방마다 보석이 철철 넘친다고 합니다."

착한 흥부가 부자가 되었다는 말에 마당쇠는 신이 나서 침을 튀기며 말했어요. 하지만 놀부는 아무리 생각해도 그 소문이 믿기지 않았어요.

> 침을 튀기다: Used when someone speaks passionately.

'불쌍한 사람을 만나면 제가 먹을 밥까지 퍼 주던 흥부가 돈을 모아 부자가 되기는 어려울 텐데. 그럼 도둑질로 재산을 모았나? 아니면 도깨비방망이라도 주웠나? 아니야, 뜬소문일 거야.'

> **TIP!** It is said that if you wave the magic bat carried by a goblin, your wishes will come true. This often appears in old stories.

놀부는 이리저리 왔다갔다하며 고개를 저었어요. 그런데 놀부 아내도 그 소문을 듣고 참을 수 없었어요.

소문 rumor | 꽉꽉 squeezed, stuffed full | 철철 to the brim | 넘치다 to overflow | 도둑질 theft | 도깨비방망이 goblin's magic bat | 뜬소문 false rumor | 고개를 젓다 to shake one's head

"아이고 배야, 배 아파서 못 살겠네.
여보, 어서 가서 사실인지 알아보고
와요."

> 배 아프다: Indicates feeling cross because someone else is doing well.
> 예 사촌이 땅을 사면 배가 아프다

놀부는 여기저기에 흥부가 사는 동네가 어디인지 물었어요.
마침내 흥부의 집에 도착했더니 겉모습만 봐도 입이 딱 벌어질
정도였어요. 임금이 사는 집이 이보다 더 좋을까요?

"이놈, 흥부야!"

놀부가 있는 힘껏 소리를 질렀어요. 흥부네 부부는 버선발로 달려
나와 놀부를 맞이했어요.

> 버선발로 나오다: Indicates that the subject is in such a hurry that they run outside without putting their shoes on.

"어서 오십시오. 형님!"

"아주버님, 그동안 잘 지내셨어요?"

놀부는 인사도 받지 않고 소리부터 질러 댔어요.

"이놈 흥부야, 도대체 도둑질을 얼마나 많이 했길래 이렇게 부자가
되었느냐?"

흥부는 무슨 일인지 몰랐지만 형님을 진정시키기 위해 노력했어요.
놀부는 흥부가 어떻게 부자가 되었는지 빨리 듣고 싶었지만,
형 체면에 바로 물을 수도 없어 괜히 불평을 늘어놓았어요.

"너는 조상을 잘 만나 부자가 되었으면 이 형을 찾아와야지,
어떻게 이리 발길을 딱 끊고 살았느냐?"

> 발(길)을 끊다: Indicates the cutting off of a relationship or contact.

겉모습 appearance | 힘껏 with all one's might | 아주버님 one's husband's older brother |
소리를 지르다 to shout | 진정시키다 to calm someone down | 괜히 in vain, for no reason |
불평을 늘어놓다 to make complaints

"저 또한 형님을 찾아뵙고 인사드리고 싶었지만, 형님께서 다시는 눈앞에 나타나지 말라고 하셔서 망설이고 있었습니다."

놀부는 흥부에게 어떻게 부자가 되었는지 다시 물었고 흥부는 지난봄부터 있었던 일을 자세히 이야기했어요. 놀부는 흥부의 말을 듣고 속으로 만세를 불렀어요.

급한 마음에 서둘러 일어서던 놀부는 마루에 놓인 옷장에 눈길이 멈추었어요. 한눈에 꽤 값이 나가는 물건 같았어요.

"저것 좋아 보이는구나. 나에게 선물로 주면 좋겠다."

"네, 그럼 제가 하인들을 시켜 형님네로 보내 드리겠습니다."

놀부는 혹시라도 하인들이 옮기다가 부서지기라도 할까 봐 혼자서 끙끙대며 집까지 가져갔어요.

망설이다 to hesitate | 만세를 부르다 to cheer, to shout hurrah | 마루 floor | 눈길 eyes, gaze | 꽤 quite, rather | 옮기다 to move | 부서지다 to break | 끙끙대다 to groan, to struggle

놀부는 집에 도착해 옷장을 내려놓으면서 흥부에게 들은 이야기를 아내에게 들려주었어요. 놀부의 말이 끝나자마자 놀부 아내는 방바닥을 구르기 시작했어요.

"아이고, 흥부가 벼락부자가 되었다는 소문이 진짜였구나! 아이고, 배가 아파 못 살겠네."

> 벼락부자: Indicates a person who suddenly earned a large amount of money or became rich.

아내에게 놀부가 작은 소리로 말했어요.

"부인, 나한테 좋은 방법이 있소. 우리도 제비 잡으러 갑시다!"

그 말을 들은 놀부 아내의 얼굴에는 웃음이 가득했어요. 그리고 방문을 활짝 열며 큰 소리로 말했어요.

"하하하, 제비야 우리 집으로 날아오너라."

방바닥 floor | 구르다 to roll

7

제비 잡으러 나가는 놀부

Track 07

그날 이후 놀부와 놀부 아내는 봄이 되기만을 눈이 빠지게
기다렸어요. 마침내 봄이
돌아왔어요. 그렇게 기다리던

> 눈이 빠지게 기다리다: Indicates waiting for an extremely long period of time.

제비 한 쌍이 놀부네 처마 밑에 집을 지었어요. 놀부와 놀부 아내는
벌써 보물이 나오는 박씨를 얻은 것처럼 기뻐 춤을 추었어요.
그때부터 놀부 부부는 누가 훔쳐 갈까 두려워 처마 아래쪽에 앉아
제비 집을 지켰지요.

다행히 놀부네 지붕에서 제비가 알을 다섯 개 낳았어요. 놀부는
너무 좋아서 매일 사다리를 타고 올라가 제비 알을 만졌어요. 그런데
놀부가 하도 알을 만지는 바람에 다른 알은 다 상하거나 깨지고 딱
한 개만 남았어요. 그 알에서 새끼 제비 한 마리가 깨어 났어요.

"이제는 저 제비가 다리만 부러지면 되겠구나!"

그런데 이것도 제비를 기다리는 것만큼이나 힘들고 지루했어요.
그래서 하인들에게 커다란 구렁이를 잡아 오게 했어요. 그리고 그
구렁이를 제비 집이 있는 쪽에 놓아 주었어요.

한 쌍 one pair | 두렵다 to be afraid of | 사다리를 타다 to climb a ladder | 하도 too much, so much
(that) | 상하다 to spoil, to go bad, to be hurt | 깨어나다 to wake up

'구렁이가 제비 집을 공격해야 놀란 새끼 제비가 떨어져 다리를 다칠 거야.'

이렇게 생각한 놀부는 막대기로 구렁이를 제비 쪽으로 몰았어요. 놀부가 자꾸 막대기로 머리를 치자 구렁이는 놀부를 공격했어요. 놀부는 놀라서 도망치다가 좋은 방법을 생각해 냈어요. 놀부는 사다리를 타고 제비 집으로 올라가서 잠든 제비의 다리를 순식간에 '뚝' 하고 부러뜨렸어요. 그리고 큰 소리로 슬프게 울었어요.

"아이고, 불쌍해서 어쩌나. 나쁜 구렁이를 피해 도망치다가 제비 다리가 부러졌구나. 흑흑."

공격하다 to attack | 몰다 to steer, to drive (toward) | 순식간 in an instant | 부러뜨리다 to break, to fracture

제비 다리가 부러졌다는 소리에 놀부 아내는 낮잠에서 깨어 콧노래를 불렀어요. 그리고는 제비 다리를 치료하며 이렇게 말했어요.

"경사 났네, 경사 났어!"

제비는 울면서 강남으로 돌아가 제비 임금님께 이 사실을 알렸어요. 제비 임금님은 박씨 하나를 또 주었어요. 다시 봄이 되어 제비가 박씨를 물고 놀부 집으로 돌아오자 놀부 부부는 신이 나서 어쩔 줄 몰랐어요.

"제비야. 어디 갔다가 이제야 왔느냐. 지난해에 부러진 다리를 고쳐 주었으니 은혜를 잊지 않았다면 어서 박씨를 내놓아라."

제비가 입에 물었던 박씨를 놀부 부부의 손바닥에 떨어뜨렸어요. 놀부는 바로 햇빛이 잘 드는 곳에 박씨를 심었어요. 얼마 지나지 않아 박씨가 무럭무럭 자라 커다란 박이 열 통이나 열렸어요.

"흥부 놈은 겨우 네 통으로 벼락부자가 되었는데 나는 열 통이나 열렸으니 얼마나 많을까? 그 돈을 다 어떻게 쓸까?"

놀부는 부자가 될 생각에 신이 나 덩실덩실 춤을 추었어요.

콧노래 humming | **경사** happy occasion | **내놓다** to put out, to take out | **햇빛이 들다** to be sunlit

8

박 자르는 놀부네

Track 08

드디어 놀부가 큰 박 하나를 톱으로 자르기 시작했어요.

"슬근슬근 톱질하세. 슬근슬근 톱질하세. 금은보화 비단옷에 온갖 보물 쏟아져라."

하지만 아무리 톱질을 해도 돌처럼 단단해서 자를 수가 없었어요. 마당쇠를 불러와 톱질을 시켜도 똑같았어요. 그래서 힘이 센 일꾼을 따로 불러서 박을 잘랐어요.

쩍! 드디어 박 한 통이 천둥 같은 소리를 내면서 갈라졌어요. 그런데 나오라는 보물은 안 나오고 한 노인이 수염을 쓰다듬으며 걸어 나오는 거예요. 그러더니 바로 놀부에게 소리쳤어요.

"네 이놈 놀부야, 네 할아버지의 할아버지가 내게 빚진 삼 천냥을 언제 갚을 것이냐?"

놀부는 노인의 말에 코웃음을 쳤어요. 놀부가 이름도 모르는 조상이 진 빚을 그냥 갚아 줄 리가 없지요.

> V + -(으)ㄹ 리가 없다: Indicates the speaker's certainty that the contents of the preceding clause cannot be a reason or have no possibility of happening.

금은보화 gold and silver treasure | 단단하다 to be hard, to be solid | 일꾼 worker, manual laborer | 천둥 thunder | 수염 mustache, beard | 쓰다듬다 to stroke | 빚지다 to be in debt

"얘들아, 어서 나와 놀부 놈을 혼내 주어라!"

노인의 말이 끝나자 박 속에서 사람들이 몰려나와 놀부를
나무 위에 매달았어요. 놀부는 삼천 냥을 주고 나서야 내려올 수
있었어요. 놀부는 빼앗긴 돈이 아까워 숨도 잘 못 쉬었어요. 하지만
아직 박이 많이 남았다고 스스로 위로하며 다시 박을 잘랐어요.

쩍! 두 번째 박이 갈라지자 이번에는 목탁 소리가 들리며 한
스님이 나타났어요.

"이놈, 놀부야, 우리가 너를 위해 부처님께 빌고 또 빌었는데
아직까지 빈손이라니 더는 안 되겠다."

> **V + -라니:** Used when repeating a question or wondering in surprise after hearing something unexpected.

그 말에 놀부는 얼른 안방에서 돈
천 냥을 꺼내 와서 스님에게 드렸어요.
오천 냥은 있어야 한다는 스님 말에 스님의 박 속에 돈을 넣고 또
넣었어요. 그런데 이상하게도 돈이 들어가기만 하면 연기처럼
사라지는 거예요.

놀부는 너무 화가 났지만, 다시 세 번째 박을 잘라 보기로 했어요.
그러자 이번에는 거지들이 나와서는 자기네 집 마당처럼 덩실덩실
춤을 췄어요.

"놀부의 인심이 좋다는 말을 듣고 일부러 찾아왔으니 실컷 놀고
갑시다."

혼내다 to scold, to teach someone a lesson | 몰려나오다 to spill out, to pour out | 매달다 to hang up,
to suspend | 목탁 moktak (wooden instrument used by Buddhist monks) | 스님 monk |
부처님 Buddha | 인심 one's heart

그러고는 쌀 내놔라, 술 내놔라, 돈 내놔라 하며 떠들어 댔어요.
거지들이 재산을 다 없앨까 봐 걱정이 된 놀부는 돈과 쌀을 주면서
거지들을 쫓아냈어요. 이번에는 진짜 보물이 들어 있을 거라고
믿으면서 박을 하나씩 잘랐지만 계속해서 무서운 일만 일어났어요.

쩍! 아홉 번째 박 속에서 나온 사람들이 망치와 도끼를 들고
놀부와 놀부 아내를 마구 때렸어요. 자세히 보니 그 사람들은 앞을
못 보거나, 몸이 불편했는데 모두 놀부에게 당한 사람들이었어요.
그들을 간신히 달랬지만 그나마 있던 땅문서도 모두 빼앗기고
말았어요.

쫓아내다 to kick out, to chase away | **망치** hammer | **도끼** axe, hatchet | **마구** violently, severely |
그나마 even so, nevertheless | **땅문서** land registry certificate

일꾼들은 더 무서운 일이 일어날까 봐 도망가 버리고 놀부 아내는 사라진 돈이 아까워 땅을 치며 울었어요. 이제 하나 남은 박을 자르는 것도 무서웠어요.

> 땅을 치다: Used to describe feeling victimized and very upset.

그래도 놀부는 그 박 속에서 어쩌면 보물이 나올지도 모른다는 기대를 버릴 수 없었어요.

"이제 줄 것도 없으니 속는 셈 치고 잘라 봅시다."

두 사람은 힘을 합쳐 남은 박 하나를 잘랐어요.

> 속는 셈 치다: Means that the subject thinks they are being deceived and taking a chance.

"슬근슬근 톱질하세, 금도 좋다, 은도 좋다. 많이만 나오너라."

박이 조금씩 갈라지는데 그 속이 노란색으로 빛났어요. 이번에는 진짜 금인 것 같았어요. 조금 이상한 냄새가 났지만 노란 빛을 보자 저절로 힘이 났어요.

'찍!' 하는 소리와 함께 박 속에서 노란 똥물이 콸콸 흘러나와 집 전체를 가득 채워 버렸어요.

"아이고, 놀부 살려."

놀부는 똥물에 빠져 살려 달라고 소리를 질렀어요. 그러나 아무도 도와주지 않았어요. 놀부 부부는 간신히 헤엄쳐서 밖으로 나왔어요.

순식간에 집도 재산도 모두 잃어버린 놀부 부부는 온몸에 똥을 가득 묻힌 채 흥부네 집을 향해 걸어갔어요.

기대 expectation, anticipation | 빛나다 to shine | 저절로 naturally, automatically | 콸콸 gushing, profusely | 흘러나오다 to gush out | 채우다 to fill | 똥물 waste (excrement) water | 묻히다 to be covered

9
사이좋은 형제

Track 09

엉망인 모습으로 나타난 형을 보고 흥부는 급히 달려 나갔어요.

"형님, 형님, 이게 무슨 일이에요? 어서 들어가십시다."

흥부는 놀부 부부와 조카들을 데리고 집으로 들어왔어요.

"형님, 아무 걱정하지 마시고 편히 쉬십시오."

흥부는 서둘러 안방에 형님 부부를 머물게 한 다음, 먹을 것과 입을 것을 대접하며 위로하였어요. 얼마 후에는 좋은 곳을 찾아 자기 집만큼 크고 좋은 집을 지어 주었어요. 게다가 살림살이, 옷, 음식도 자기와 똑같이 준비해 주었어요.

"흥부야, 정말 고맙구나!"

비록 놀부는 나쁜 놈이었으나 흥부의 착한 마음에 감동하여 과거의 잘못을 반성하고 서로 사이좋게 지냈어요.

그 뒤 흥부는 오랫동안 행복하게 잘 살았고 자손들도 모두 건강하게 부를 누렸어요. 세상 사람들이 흥부의 덕을 칭찬하여 그 이름이 오랫동안 사람들의 기억 속에 남았다고 해요.

사이좋다 to be close, to be friendly | **엉망이다** to be a wreck | **조카** niece, nephew | **머물다** to stay
대접하다 to treat someone to something | **자손** descendant | **부를 누리다** to enjoy wealth | **덕** virtue

부록
Appendix

● 내용 이해하기
  Reading Comprehension

● 모범 답안
  Answers

● 본문 번역
  Text Translations

1

1 빈칸에 알맞은 단어를 넣어 대화를 완성하세요.

Put the correct word in each blank to complete the dialogues.

| 몫 | 이웃 | 심술 | 체면 |

(1) 가 (   ) 차리지 말고 많이 드세요.

　　나 네, 감사합니다. 잘 먹겠습니다.

(2) 가 피자를 시켰는데 네 (   )(으)로 몇 조각 남겨 두었어.

　　나 고마워, 역시 누나밖에 없네.

(3) 가 형이 방을 정리하지 않아서 청소할 때 형 물건을 전부 다 버렸어요.

　　나 정말? 너는 왜 그렇게 형에게 (   )을/를 부려?

(4) 가 이사는 잘했어요?

　　나 네, 정리를 다 했고요. 이제 (   )에게 인사를 다닐까 해요.

2 빈칸에 알맞은 단어를 넣어 문장을 완성하세요.

Put the correct word in each blank to complete the sentences.

| 유언 | 살다 | 굶다 | 내쫓다 |

(1) 놀부는 흥부를 (   ) 재산을 혼자 가지려 했다.

(2) 경상도와 전라도 사이에 연 생원이 (   ) 있었다.

(3) 병을 앓던 연 생원은 마지막 (   )을/를 남기고 죽었다.

(4) 하루 종일 (   ) 아이들은 아침부터 밥 달라고 울었다.

3 이야기의 내용과 맞으면 'O', 틀리면 'x' 표시하세요.

Mark ○ if the statement is true, and mark × if it is false.

(1) 놀부와 흥부는 서로 사이가 좋았다. ( )

(2) 아버지는 흥부에게 대부분의 재산을 남겼다. ( )

(3) 놀부는 흥부의 재산을 모두 빼앗고 내쫓았다. ( )

(4) 놀부는 아버지가 돌아가시자 동생을 잘 돌봐주었다. ( )

4 다음 중 놀부가 한 일이 아닌 것은 무엇입니까?

Which of the following is not something that Nolbu did?

① 호박에 말뚝 박기 ② 우물곁에 똥 누기

③ 불난 데 부채질하기 ④ 추운 사람 옷 벗어 주기

5 다음 질문에 알맞은 답을 쓰세요.

Write the correct answer for each of the following questions.

(1) 놀부와 흥부의 성격은 어떻게 다른가요?

① 놀부: _____

② 흥부: _____

(2) 연 생원이 죽기 전에 한 유언은 무엇인가요?

_____

_____

(3) 놀부가 흥부를 내쫓으려는 이유는 무엇인가요?

_____

_____

<u>2</u>

1 빈칸에 알맞은 단어를 넣어 대화를 완성하세요.
Put the correct word in each blank to complete the dialogues.

| 끼니 | 고생 | 실컷 | 말리다 |

(1) 가 ( ) 끝에 드디어 빌린 돈을 다 갚았어요.

　　나 우와, 열심히 일하더니 정말 다행이네요.

(2) 가 저는 외국에서 공부하고 싶은데 부모님이 자꾸 ( ).

　　나 부모님이 반대하는 이유가 무엇인지 한번 들어보면 어때요?

(3) 가 이번 휴가 때 여행 가실 거예요?

　　나 아니요, 너무 피곤해서 집에서 ( ) 자려고요.

(4) 가 사장님, 지금처럼 성공하기 전에 많이 힘드셨다고 들었어요.

　　나 네, ( )을/를 거르는 일도 많을 정도였어요.

2 흥부는 다음 사람들을 어떻게 부르나요? 알맞은 호칭을 연결하세요.
What would Heungbu call the following people? Connect each person with the appropriate title.

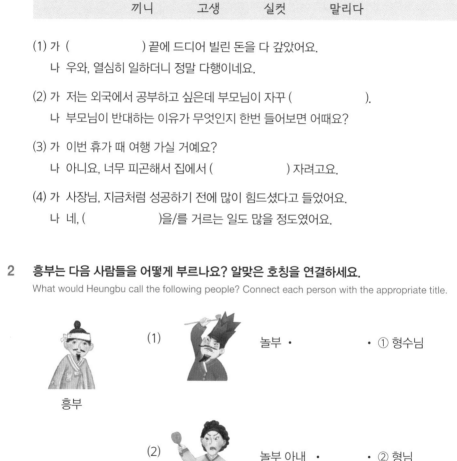

흥부

(1) 놀부 ・　　　　　・ ① 형수님

(2) 놀부 아내 ・　　　　　・ ② 형님

3 다음 그림에 알맞은 단어를 골라 쓰세요.

Choose and write the correct word for each of the following pictures.

| 몽둥이 | 부지깽이 | 담뱃대 | 주걱 |

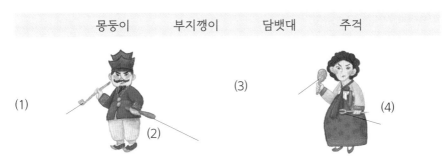

(1)

(2)

(3)

(4)

4 빈칸에 알맞은 단어를 넣어 문장을 완성하세요.

Put the correct word in each blank to complete the sentences.

| 밥풀 | 피붙이 | 사정없이 | 피하다 |

(1) 흥부는 몽둥이를 (　　　　　　) 부엌에 들어갔다.

(2) 흥부는 너무 배가 고파서 뺨에 붙은 (　　　　　　)을/를 얼른 먹었다.

(3) 도와달라는 흥부의 말에 놀부는 (　　　　　　) 담뱃대를 던졌다.

(4) 놀부는 자기는 (　　　　　　) 하나 없다며 먹을 것을 얻으러 온 흥부를 모른 척했다.

5 다음 질문에 알맞은 답을 쓰세요.

Write the correct answer for each of the following questions.

(1) 밥을 달라는 자식들을 보며 흥부 아내는 흥부에게 무슨 말을 했나요?

_____

_____

(2) 마당쇠는 매를 때리는 놀부를 말릴 수 없었어요. 그 이유는 무엇인가요?

_____

_____

<u>3</u>

1 빈칸에 알맞은 단어를 넣어 글을 완성하세요.

Put the correct word in each blank to complete the text.

잔뜩	조심스럽다	서운하다	비록	풀어 주다

집에 돌아와 보니 룸메이트의 기분이 안 좋아 보였다. (1) (   )게
무슨 일인지 물어보니 친한 친구에게 (2) (   ) 일이 있었다고 했다.
(3) (   ) 속상한 얼굴을 한 룸메이트의 기분을 (4) (   )
기 위해 오랫동안 대화했다. (5) (   ) 조금 피곤했지만 룸메이트의
기분이 나아진 것 같아 다행이었다.

2 다음 중 흥부가 한 일로 알맞은 것은 무엇입니까?

Which of the following is something that Heungbu did?

① 도적과 싸웠다.

② 죄인 대신 매를 맞았다.

③ 관청에서 곡식을 빌렸다.

④ 한겨울에 농사를 지었다.

3 일이 일어난 순서에 맞게 쓰세요.

Order the events by writing their numbers.

① 흥부는 매를 대신 맞기로 하고 관청 직원에게 돈을 받아 왔다.

② 흥부는 놀부에 대해 나쁘게 말하지 않으려고 도둑을 만났다고 말했다.

③ 정화수를 떠 놓고 빌던 흥부 아내는 흥부를 보고 활짝 웃었다.

④ 나라에 좋은 일이 생겨 흥부는 빈손으로 집으로 돌아갔다.

⑤ 흥부와 흥부 아내는 돈을 벌기 위해서 무슨 일이든 했지만 먹고살기 힘들었다.

_____ → _____ → _____ → _____ → _____

4 다음 질문에 알맞은 답을 쓰세요.

Write the correct answer for each of the following questions.

(1) 대신 매를 맞아 돈을 벌겠다는 흥부에게 아내는 무슨 말을 했나요?

_____

_____

_____

(2) 김 영감의 아들이 흥부를 찾아온 이유는 무엇인가요?

_____

_____

4

1 그림을 보고 알맞은 단어를 쓰고 문장을 만드세요.

Write the word that best describes each illustration, and then complete the sentences.

(1) 봄이 되자 (　　　　　　)이/가 흥부 집에 날아왔다.

(2) 어느 날 (　　　　　　)이/가 나타나 새끼 제비 한 마리만 남기고 모두 잡아먹었다.

(3) 제비 나라 임금님은 제비에게 (　　　　　　)을/를 주어 흥부에게 은혜를 갚도록 했다.

(4) 흥부는 제비가 준 박씨를 (　　　　　　) 밑에 심었다.

2 빈칸에 알맞은 단어를 넣어 문장을 완성하세요.

Put the correct word in each blank to complete the sentences.

점점	뚝딱	포르르	덩실덩실

(1) 놀란 제비가 (　　　　　　) 날아올랐다.

(2) 제비를 보자 흥부는 (　　　　　　) 춤을 추었다.

(3) 제비 부부는 (　　　　　　) 집 한 채를 만들었다.

(4) 날은 (　　　　　　) 따뜻해지고 꽃 피는 봄이 되었다.

3 어울리는 것끼리 연결하여 문장을 완성하세요.
Connect the phrases that go together to create complete sentences.

(1) 제비가 처마 밑에 집을
      짓자 아이들은 기뻐했지만 ·

· ① 제비의 오른쪽 다리가
      부러져 있었어요.

(2) 흥부가 자세히 살펴보니 ·

· ② 흥부는 자식이 온 것처럼
      기뻤어요.

(3) 우리 집 처마를 비워 둘 테니 ·

· ③ 흥부는 제비가 불쌍했어요.

(4) 제비가 돌아오자 ·

· ④ 내년에 꼭 돌아오너라.

4 다음 질문에 알맞은 답을 쓰세요.
Write the correct answer for each of the following questions.

(1) 흥부는 다친 새끼 제비를 어떻게 했나요?

_____

_____

(2) 흥부가 살려준 제비는 임금님께 어떤 소원을 말했나요?

_____

_____

(3) 제비는 흥부에게 줄 박씨를 어떻게 가져왔나요?

_____

_____

<u>5</u>

1 다음 문장에 어울리는 단어를 찾아 ○ 표시하세요.
Circle the word that best suits each of the following sentences.

(1) 갑자기 박이 (쩍 , 딱) 갈라지고 그 속에서 사내아이가 나왔다.

(2) 흥부와 흥부의 아내는 (마주, 바로) 앉아 톱질을 하기 시작했어요.

(3) (보름달, 반달) 같은 박에서 온갖 보물이 (쏟아졌다, 사라졌다).

(4) 흥부와 흥부 아내는 귀신에 (홀린, 낚인) 듯 정신이 하나도 없었어요.

2 다음 중 박에서 나온 것으로 알맞은 것을 연결하세요.
Connect each of the following with the correct gourd out of which it came.

(1) 첫 번째 박 •
                   • ① 집안일을 돕는 사람들

                   • ② 병과 약초

(2) 두 번째 박 •

                   • ③ 보물

(3) 세 번째 박 •

                   • ④ 쌀과 돈이 든 상자

(4) 네 번째 박 •
                   • ⑤ 집을 짓는 사람들

3 빈칸에 알맞은 신체 부위를 넣어 문장을 완성하세요.

Put the correct body part in each blank to complete the sentences.

코 　 입 　 귀 　 눈 　 배

(1) (　　　　　) 깜짝할 사이에 기와집 한 채가 생겨났다.

(2) 어찌나 많이 먹었는지 (　　　　　)이/가 터질 것 같았다.

(3) 추석이 가까워지자 다른 집에서는 음식 냄새가 (　　　　　)을/를 찔렀다.

(4) 놀라서 (　　　　　)이/가 딱 벌어진 아내에게 흥부가 기쁜 목소리로 말했어요.

4 다음 질문에 알맞은 답을 쓰세요.

Write the correct answer for each of the following questions.

(1) 흥부는 왜 박을 자르려고 했나요?

_____

_____

(2) 흥부의 아내는 흥부네가 부자가 된 이유를 무엇이라고 생각했나요?

_____

_____

6

1 빈칸에 알맞은 단어를 넣어 문장을 완성하세요.

Put the correct word in each blank to complete the sentences.

신	소문	불평	버선발

(1) 놀부가 찾아오자 흥부는 (　　　　　)(으)로 달려 나왔다.

(2) 흥부가 부자가 되었다는 (　　　　　)이/가 놀부 귀에까지 들어왔다.

(3) 형 체면에 바로 물을 수 없어 (　　　　　)을/를 늘어놓았다.

(4) 마당쇠는 착한 흥부가 부자가 되었다는 말에 (　　　　　)이/가 났다.

2 상황에 알맞은 표현을 찾아 연결하세요.

Connect each situation with the appropriate expression.

(1)　착한 흥부가 부자가 되었다는
　　사실을 마당쇠가 놀부에게 전할 때　　　　·

　　　　·　① 입이 딱 벌어지다

(2)　놀부 부부가 흥부가 부자가
　　되었다는 사실을 확인한 후　　　　·

　　　　·　② 침을 튀기며 말하다

(3)　놀부가 대궐 같은 흥부 집을
　　처음 보았을 때　　　　·

　　　　·　③ 사촌이 땅을 사면
　　　　　배가 아프다

3 '흥부가 부자가 되었다'는 소문을 들은 놀부가 생각한 것이 <u>아닌</u> 것은?

Which of the following is not one of Nolbu's thoughts upon hearing the rumor that Heungbu had become a wealthy man?

① 뜬소문일 것이다.　　　　　② 도깨비방망이를 주웠다.

③ 도둑질로 재산을 모았다.　　　④ 제비가 도와주었을 것이다.

4 놀부가 흥부 집에서 가져온 물건은 무엇입니까?

What is the item that Nolbu took from Heungbu's house?

① 옷장   ② 화장대

③ 보석   ④ 제비집

5 다음 중 인물의 감정을 나타내는 행동이 잘못 쓰인 것은 무엇입니까?

Which of the following sentences incorrectly describes the character's behavior showing their emotions?

① 놀부는 흥부 집 마루에 놓인 옷장을 가져가고 싶어서 고개를 저었다.

② 드디어 흥부가 어떻게 부자가 되었는지 알게 된 놀부는 속으로 만세를 불렀다.

③ 놀부는 흥부가 부자가 되었다는 말을 듣고 고민하며 이리저리 왔다 갔다 했다.

④ 놀부의 아내는 흥부가 부자가 되었다는 말을 듣고 배가 아프다며 방바닥을 굴렀다.

6 다음 질문에 알맞은 답을 쓰세요.

Write the correct answer for each of the following questions.

(1) 놀부의 이야기를 듣고 놀부 아내가 방바닥을 구른 이유가 무엇인가요?

_____

_____

(2) 부자가 된 흥부가 형 놀부를 찾아가지 않은 이유는 무엇인가요?

_____

_____

<u>7</u>

1 다음 중 <u>틀린</u> 부분을 찾아 알맞게 고치세요.

Find and correct the mistakes in the following sentences.

(1) 놀부 부부는 봄이 되기만을 눈이 힘들게 기다렸다.

(→   )

(2) 제비 한 쌍이 놀부 집 처마 밑에 집을 지켰다.

(→   )

(3) 놀부는 자기 손으로 새끼 제비의 다리를 떨어뜨렸다.

(→   )

(4) 다시 봄이 되어 제비가 박씨를 타고 놀부 집으로 돌아왔다.

(→   )

(5) 얼마 지나지 않아 박씨가 덩실덩실 자라 커다란 박이 열렸다.

(→   )

2 이야기의 내용과 맞으면 ○, 틀리면 × 표시하세요.

Mark ○ if the statement is true, and mark × if it is false.

(1) 제비 알 다섯 개는 모두 구렁이 때문에 상하거나 깨졌다.   (   )

(2) 놀부는 직접 구렁이를 잡아 와서 제비 집이 있는 쪽에 놓아 주었다.   (   )

(3) 놀부 아내는 제비 다리를 치료하며 신이 났다.   (   )

(4) 놀부가 제비의 다리를 부러뜨렸다고 해서 임금님은 박씨를 주지 않았다.   (   )

(5) 놀부가 심은 박씨가 자라 커다란 박 열 통이 열렸다.   (   )

3 누구의 생각입니까? 알맞게 연결하세요.

Which character had each of the following thoughts? Connect each character to the correct thought.

(1) 놀부 • · ① '이 박씨로 놀부를 혼내 줘야겠다.'

(2) 놀부 아내 • · ② '구렁이가 있어야 제비 다리가 부러질 거야.'

(3) 제비 • · ③ '내가 치료해 줄게, 어서 박씨를 가져와라.'

(4) 임금님 • · ④ '놀부의 나쁜 행동을 어서 알려야지.'

4 다음 질문에 알맞은 답을 쓰세요.

Write the correct answer for each of the following questions.

(1) 놀부 집 처마 밑에 있던 제비는 왜 다리가 부러졌나요?

_____

_____

(2) 제비 다리가 부러졌을 때 놀부 아내가 한 말은 무엇인가요?

_____

_____

(3) 다시 돌아온 제비를 보고 놀부가 한 말은 무엇인가요?

_____

_____

8

1 다음 중 관계가 나머지와 <u>다른</u> 것은 무엇입니까?

Which of the following word pairs has a different relationship than the other word pairs?

① 단단하다 – 부드럽다   ② 나타나다 – 사라지다

③ 빚을 지다 – 빚을 갚다   ④ 톱질하다 – 자르다

2 빈칸에 알맞은 단어를 넣어 문장을 완성하세요.

Put the correct word in each blank to complete the sentences.

스님	돌	조상들	거지들

(1) 박이 ( )처럼 단단해서 놀부는 힘센 일꾼을 불렀디.

(2) 두 번째 박에서 나온 ( )은/는 놀부에게서 오천 냥을 가져갔다.

(3) 놀부는 세 번째 박에서 나온 ( )에게 돈 백 냥과 쌀 한 섬을 주어 보냈다.

(4) 첫 번째 박에서 나온 노인과 젊은이들은 ( )이/가 진 빚 삼천 냥을 놀부에게서 빼앗아 갔다.

3 놀부는 재산을 다 빼앗기고 온몸이 아팠지만, 마지막 박을 자르기로 했어요. 그 이유는 무엇일까요?

Nolbu lost everything he had, and his entire body was in pain, but he decided to cut open the last gourd. What was his reason for doing this?

① 착해서   ② 욕심이 많아서

③ 화가 나서   ④ 제비한테 속아서

4 누구의 생각입니까? 알맞게 연결하세요.

Which character had each of the following thoughts? Connect each character to the correct thought.

(1) 놀부 부부 •

• ① '다음 박에선 더 무서운 일이 생길 거야'

(2) 일꾼들 •

• ② '다음 박에는 반드시 보물이 나올 거야'

5 다음 질문에 알맞은 답을 쓰세요.

Write the correct answer for each of the following questions.

(1) 마지막 박을 자르며 놀부는 진짜 금이 나올 거라고 생각했어요. 그렇게 생각한 까닭은 무엇인가요?

_____

_____

(2) 마지막 박에서 나온 것은 무엇인가요?

_____

_____

(3) 집도 재산도 모두 잃은 놀부 부부는 어떻게 했나요?

_____

_____

<u>9</u>

1 빈칸에 알맞은 단어를 넣어 문장을 완성하세요.

Put the correct word in each blank to complete the sentences.

덕	똑같이	망하다	뉘우치다

(1) 흥부는 형 놀부가 (　　　　　　) 소식을 들었다.

(2) 세상 사람들이 흥부의 (　　　　　　)을/를 칭찬하였다.

(3) 흥부의 착한 마음에 감동한 놀부는 잘못을 (　　　　　).

(4) 흥부는 놀부에게 집도 살림살이도 의복도 (　　　　　) 나눠 주었다.

2 다음은 흥부가 한 일입니다. 글의 내용에 맞게 순서대로 나열하세요.

The following are things that Heungbu did in the story. Arrange them in the correct order.

① 오랫동안 행복하게 잘 살았다.
② 놀부 가족이 살 집을 지어 주었다.
③ 모습이 엉망인 놀부를 보고 급히 달려 나갔다.
④ 놀부에게 먹을 것과 입을 것을 주며 위로했다.
⑤ 놀부 부부와 조카들을 집으로 데리고 들어왔다.

→ _____ → _____ → _____ → _____ → _____

3 흥부의 생각으로 알맞지 <u>않은</u> 것을 고르세요.

Which of the following is not something Heungbu thought?

① 힘든 일을 겪은
형이 안쓰러워요.

② 형과 사이좋게 지내게
되어서 기뻐요.

③ 형이 편하게 살 수 있게
돕고 싶어요.

④ 그동안 형에게 나쁘게
행동한 것이 미안해요.

4 다음 중 글의 내용과 <u>다른</u> 것은 무엇입니까?

Choose the answer that does not match the content of the story.

① 놀부는 자신의 잘못을 반성했다.

② 놀부는 흥부의 착한 마음에 감동했다.

③ 세상 사람들은 흥부의 덕을 칭찬했다.

④ 놀부와 흥부는 오랫동안 한 집에서 함께 살았다.

5 다음 질문에 알맞은 답을 쓰세요.

Write the correct answer for each of the following questions.

(1) 흥부가 놀부를 집에 데려와서 한 말은 무엇인가요?

_____

(2) "흥부야, 정말 고맙구나!"라는 말을 할 정도로 놀부의 마음이 변한 이유는 무엇인가요?

_____

1 ~ 9

1 보기와 같이 주어진 어휘를 사용하여 내용을 요약하세요.

Summarize the story by using the given vocabulary words, as seen in the example.

> **보기** 아버지, 돌아가시다, 형, 놀부, 동생, 흥부, 쫓아내다
> 아버지가 돌아가시자 형 놀부는 동생 흥부를 쫓아냈다.

(1) 놀부, 부자, 흥부, 힘들다, 살다

_____

(2) 어느 날, 흥부, 다치다, 제비, 다리, 치료하다

_____

(3) 제비, 선물, 주다, 박씨, 흥부, 부자, 되다

_____

(4) 욕심, 많다, 놀부, 제비, 다리, 일부러, 부러뜨리다, 고쳐 주다

_____

(5) 놀부, 제비, 박씨, 얻다, 박, 나오다, 사람들, 놀부, 재산, 모두, 빼앗다,

_____

(6) 흥부, 거지, 되다, 놀부, 도와주다, 놀부, 자신, 잘못, 반성하다

_____

2 놀부와 흥부가 한 행동 중 가장 인상 깊었던 것을 표시하고 그 행동에 대한 자신의 생각과 느낌을 말하세요.

Mark the actions done by Nolbu and Heungbu that made the deepest impression on you, and talk about your thoughts and feelings about that action.

놀부가 한 일

☐ 우물가에 똥을 누거나 호박에 말뚝을 박았다.

☐ 동생을 내쫓고 부모가 남긴 재산을 혼자 가졌다.

☐ 도와달라는 동생을 모르는 사람처럼 대하고 때렸다.

☐ 흥부의 값비싼 옷장을 달라고 한 후 하인들이 그것을 부술까 봐 혼자 힘들게 가져갔다.

☐ 제비 알을 깨뜨리고 일부러 제비의 다리를 부러뜨렸다.

☐ 도움이 필요하자, 자신이 나쁘게 대했던 동생에게 갔다.

흥부가 한 일

☐ 굶는 사람에게 밥을 주거나 추워하는 사람에게 옷을 벗어 주었다.

☐ 먹고 살기 어려운 형편에도 자식을 29명 낳아 길렀다.

☐ 가족이 굶자, 형의 집에 가서 먹을 것을 달라고 부탁했다.

☐ 밥을 먹고 싶어서 형수에게 주걱으로 때려 달라고 했다.

☐ 형이 서운하게 대해도 형에 대해 좋게 말했다.

☐ 가족을 위해 대신 매 맞는 일 같은 힘든 일을 하려고 했다.

☐ 튼튼하지 못한 자신의 집에 집을 짓는 제비를 불쌍하게 생각했다.

☐ 다친 새끼 제비의 다리를 치료하고 보살펴 주었다.

☐ 다시 돌아온 제비를 보고 기뻐하며 춤을 추었다.

☐ 자신에게 나쁘게 했던 형을 도와주었다.

3 "흥부전"은 '착한 사람은 복을 받고 나쁜 사람은 벌을 받는다'는 것과 '형제간의 우애'라는 교훈을 담고 있습니다. 여러분 나라에도 이러한 교훈이 담긴 이야기가 있나요? 소개해 봅시다.

"The Story of Heungbu" contains the lesson that "kind people receive good fortune, and bad people receive punishment," as well as the lesson of "brotherly love." Is there a story with these kinds of lessons in your country, too? Introduce the story.

1장

1 (1) 체면   (2) 몫
    (3) 심술   (4) 이웃

2 (1) 내쫓고   (2) 살고
    (3) 유언을   (4) 굶은

3 (1) ×   (2) ×   (3) ○   (4) ×

4 ④

5 (1) ① 부모에게 불효하고 형제간에 우애라고는
       손톱만큼도 없다.
       ② 마음씨 착하고 부모님께 잘하고 형을
       존중했다.
    (2) 양지 쪽의 땅은 흥부가 갖고 나머지는 놀부
       가 가져라. 대신 동생을 잘 돌봐 주고 지금처
       럼 한 집에서 형제가 사이좋게 살아라.
    (3) 부모가 물려준 많은 재산을 독차지하고
       싶기 때문이다.

2장

1 (1) 고생   (2) 말려요
    (3) 실컷   (4) 끼니를

2 (1) ②   (2) ①

3 (1) 담뱃대   (2) 몽둥이
    (3) 주걱   (4) 부지깽이

4 (1) 피해   (2) 밥풀을
    (3) 사정없이   (4) 피붙이

5 (1) 형님 댁에 가서 쌀 좀 얻어 오세요. 우리는
       굶어 죽어도 불쌍한 내 새끼들은 살려야
       하지 않겠어요?
    (2) 놀부를 말렸다가는 마당쇠도 쫓겨날 것이
       뻔했기 때문이다.

3장

1 (1) 조심스럽게   (2) 서운한
    (3) 잔뜩   (4) 풀어 주기

    (5) 비록

2 ④

3 ②, ⑤, ①, ④, ③

4 (1) 흥부가 매 맞고 벌어 온 돈으로는 쌀을 사서
       먹을 수 없다. 매를 맞다 죽기라도 하면 어린
       자식을 데리고 혼자 살 수 없다. 그러니 돈을
       돌려주고 없던 일로 하자고 했다.
    (2) 비록 매는 맞지 않았지만, 그 마음이 고맙다
       며 돈을 주고 갔다.

4장

1 (1) 제비가   (2) 구렁이가
    (3) 박씨를   (4) 처마

2 (1) 포르르   (2) 덩실덩실
    (3) 뚝딱   (4) 점점

3 (1) ③   (2) ①
    (3) ④   (4) ②

4 (1) 부러진 제비의 다리를 치료해 주었다.
    (2) 흥부의 가난을 없애 주고 편히 살 수 있도록
       해 주세요.
    (3) 박씨를 입에 물고 먼 길을 날아서 가져왔다.

5장

1 (1) 쩍   (2) 마주
    (3) 보름달, 쏟아졌다   (4) 홀린

2 (1) ②   (2) ③, ④
    (3) ⑤   (4) ①

3 (1) 눈   (2) 배가
    (3) 코를   (4) 입이

4 (1) 죽 한 그릇 끓일 쌀도 없었기 때문에 박을
       잘라서 국을 끓여 먹으려고
    (2) 흥부가 착하게 산 덕분에 흥부네 가족이
       복을 받는 것이라고 생각했다.

6장

1 (1) 버선발로 　　　　(2) 소문이
　　(3) 불평을 　　　　　(4) 신이

2 (1) ② 　　(2) ③ 　　(3) ①

3 ④

4 ①

5 ①

6 (1) 흥부가 부자가 되어서 심술이 났기 때문이다.
　　(2) 형 놀부가 다시는 눈앞에 나타나지 말라고
　　　했기 때문이다.

7장

1 (1) 힘들게 → 빠지게
　　(2) 지켰다 → 지었다
　　(3) 떨어뜨렸다 → 부러뜨렸다
　　(4) 타고 → 물고
　　(5) 덩실덩실 → 무럭무럭

2 (1) × 　(2) × 　(3) ○ 　(4) × 　(5) ○

3 (1) ② 　(2) ③ 　(3) ④ 　(4) ①

4 (1) 놀부가 사다리를 타고 올라가 잠든 제비의
　　　다리를 일부러 부러뜨렸기 때문이다.
　　(2) 경사 났네, 경사 났어.
　　(3) 지난해 부러진 다리를 고쳐 주었으니 은혜를
　　　잊지 않았다면 어서 박씨를 내놓아라.

8장

1 ④

2 (1) 돌 　　　　　(2) 스님은
　　(3) 각설이패 　　(4) 조상들이

3 ②

4 (1) ② 　　　　(2) ①

5 (1) 조금 이상한 냄새가 났지만 노란 빛을 보자
　　　금인 것 같았기 때문이다.

(2) 노란 똥물이 콸콸 흘러나와 집 전체를 가득
　　채워 버렸다.
(3) 온몸에 똥을 가득 묻힌 채 흥부네 집을 향해
　　걸어갔다.

9장

1 (1) 망했다는 　　　　(2) 덕을
　　(3) 뉘우쳤다 　　　　(4) 똑같이

2 ③, ⑤, ④, ②, ①

3 ④

4 ④

5 (1) 형님, 아무 걱정하지 마시고 편히 쉬십시오.
　　(2) 흥부의 착한 마음에 감동하여 지난날의 잘못
　　　을 반성했기 때문이다.

1~9장

1 (1) 놀부는 부자였지만 흥부는 힘들게 살았다.
　　(2) 어느 날, 흥부는 다친 제비의 다리를 치료해
　　　주었다.
　　(3) 제비가 선물로 준 박씨 덕분에 흥부는 부자
　　　가 되었다.
　　(4) 욕심 많은 놀부는 제비의 다리를 일부러 부
　　　러뜨리고 고쳐 주었다.
　　(5) 놀부도 제비에게서 박씨를 얻었지만 박에서
　　　나온 사람들은 놀부의 재산을 모두 빼앗았다.
　　(6) 흥부는 거지가 된 놀부를 도와주었고, 놀부
　　　는 자신의 잘못을 반성했다.

2 **예** 나는 놀부가 흥부의 값비싼 옷장을 달라고
　　한 후 하인들이 부술까 봐 걱정돼서 혼자 힘
　　들게 가져가는 장면이 인상적이었다. 욕심이
　　너무 많고 남을 믿지 못하면 오히려 더 힘들
　　어진다는 것을 알 수 있었다. 나라면 하인들
　　이 가져오는 옷장을 편하게 받았을 것 같다.

3 **예** (생략)

1

Heungbu is Cast Out

p. 11

In a village that was adjoined in the same way that Gyeongsang-do Province and Jeolla-do Province neighbor each other, there lived a man named Mr. Yeon. He was not a man of great wealth, but he owned some land that he had received from his ancestors, so he had enough to get by. This man had two sons; the older son was named Nolbu and the younger son was named Heungbu. These brothers were born to the same parents, but their personalities were very different. Heungbu had a kind heart, so he treated his parents well and respected his older brother; however, it was impossible to find even a tiny speck of concern for his parents and brother in Nolbu's heart.

People said that Nolbu's body was filled with ill-naturedness. Reader, would you like to hear about just how tremendously ill-natured he was?

He got drunk and got into fights, made bad situations even worse, slapped the cheeks of people who had done nothing wrong, defecated around wells, ruined things at the last minute, drove stakes into pumpkins, pinched young children…

p. 12

Unlike his older brother, Heungbu was praised by everyone in the neighborhood.

He greeted the neighborhood elders, got along well with his neighbors, reduced his own portions to give food to people who were hungry, took off his own clothes and gave them to people who were cold, helped lost children find their parents…

Heungbu was such a kind person that he did not even carelessly kick the stones in the street. To Nolbu, Heungbu seemed like a nuisance every time he saw him.

But one day, Mr. Yeon, who had suffered from disease for a long time, left the following will and passed away.

"My sons, it seems that I will not live much longer. The land on the sunny side of our property is Heungbu's share, and the rest belongs to Nolbu. In exchange, Nolbu, you must look after your younger brother. Even if I die, live a happy life together in this house, just as you are now."

But Nolbu did not have any intention of abiding by his father's will. Nolbu planned to cast out Heungbu and take all of the assets left by his parents for himself.

p. 13

One day, Nolbu woke up Heungbu with a shout.

"Heungbu! I hate the sight of you playing around every day with no thought of earning any money, so I can't live with you anymore. Although there is some property that our parents left behind, as the eldest son, all of that rightfully belongs to me, so not a single piece of straw can be given to you. Even if two brothers live together while they're young, it's only right for each of us to live on our own when we get married and have children. So, take your family and go someplace far away from here right this instant."

Heungbu suddenly didn't know what his brother was saying, so he just listened silently.

"It seems like you only rely on me, but I can't feed or clothe your family anymore. So get out of my house right now, and make your own living. Our father would probably think the same way."

Heungbu felt like the sky was caving in. His late father had told them to live together no matter what happened, but now that his older brother was suddenly telling him to get out of the house, Heungbu had no idea what he should do.

Heungbu prostrated himself on the ground and begged Nolbu.

"No, brother. If I suddenly have to leave with my wife and young children, where will we go? What will we eat? Please, for heaven's sake, don't say such things!"

p. 14

Nolbu grew angry and shouted.

"I don't want to hear it. Don't you even know how to be grateful to me for feeding and clothing your family until now? If you get married and have a family, of course, you should leave with them and live on your own. Get out of my sight immediately!"

Heungbu cried and screamed as he begged, but Nolbu did not even pretend to hear him.

Heungbu had no choice but to take his wife and young children and leave the house empty-handed.

"Goodness, my dear. Where will we suddenly go like this?"

p. 15

Poor Heungbu's wife hugged and carried their young children and cried as they left. But no matter how hungry they were, there was no one to give them food, and no matter how dark the night was, there was nowhere for them to sleep.

They starved for an entire day, so in the morning the children begged for food and began to cry. Heungbu no longer had anything, not even his honor. He thought that his first priority should be finding a house, and then he should do any kind of work that he could find.

2
Nolbu Refuses to Help Heungbu

p.16

From that day on, Heungbu went around continuously searching for a place to live. Finally, in a village near his hometown, he discovered an empty house that was about to collapse. Heungbu barely managed to fix up the house and provided his family with a place to live. They were able to avoid the wind and rain, but they had no way to feed themselves. Heungbu worked without being picky about the type of work he was doing, but they barely managed not to miss any meals.

Heungbu's wife also helped him and worked without resting, but living was very exhausting and difficult. These people were very poor, but they were rich with children. They had a good relationship as husband and wife, so they had a child together every year. As a result, they had 29 children altogether.

"Mom, I'm hungry."

"Mom, please give me some food."

As soon as they opened their eyes, these numerous children cried or became irritated as they begged for food or breast milk. Heungbu's wife wept with sorrow, then looked at Heungbu and spoke.

p. 17

"Dear, please, for heaven's sake, go to your well-off older brother's house and get some rice. Even if you and I starve to death, don't you think our poor children should live?"

"It's not difficult to go to my brother's house, but even if I go there, do you really think he would give me some rice?"

"Whether he gives you any rice or not is an issue for later. For now, just try going there once. At this rate, my babies will all starve to death."

Heungbu was all too reluctant to leave, but he slung a sack for carrying rice over his shoulder, and went out of the house. Finally, he arrived at Nolbu's house and went inside with a cough of "Ahem, ahem." A male servant tried to block Heungbu from entering, but he immediately recognized Heungbu and greeted him.

"My goodness, it's the young master. I didn't even recognize you."

The servant looked at Heungbu's appearance and wiped tears from his eyes. Even though Heungbu hadn't said anything, the servant could tell how much Heungbu had suffered with just one glance.

p. 18

"Is my brother in his room?"

The servant brought Heungbu to Nolbu's room, then quickly turned around.

"Young master, don't tell him that I brought you here."

Heungbu spoke in the direction of the room.

"Brother, brother, it's me, Heungbu."

At first, there was no answer, but as soon as Heungbu called his brother again, the door opened. However, Nolbu pretended not to know Heungbu and treated him like someone he was seeing for the first time.

"Who are you?"

"It's me, Heungbu. This is what I've become after leaving you and living on my own. Please regard your one and only younger brother with pity and help me."

Heungbu sank to the floor and sobbed as he spoke.

"I think you are mistaken. I am an only son, and I have no relatives at all, let alone a younger brother."

"Brother, it seems that you are angry because I did not come to greet you often, but I beg of you. My wife and young children are starving to death, so please share just a little bit of food with us, brother."

As soon as he finished speaking, Nolbu's pipe came flying at Heungbu in a frightening way. Heungbu fell backward in shock.

p. 19

"You scoundrel, I did not stockpile rice to give it to you, nor did I save money to give it to you. I wish I could give you some clothes,

but the clothes I am wearing are all that I have, so I cannot give them to you. So, go somewhere else to look for help."

"Brother, please, give me some rice even if it is cold."

When Heungbu did not leave, Nolbu took up a rod and mercilessly beat Heungbu. The servant, who was watching nearby, anxiously stamped his feet, but he only fretted and could not stop Nolbu. He was nearly thrown out himself after trying to stop Nolbu. Heungbu avoided the rod and escaped, then rushed into the kitchen.

At that very moment, Nolbu's wife was scooping out some rice with a rice paddle. As soon as Heungbu, who had not eaten for several days, smelled the savory scent of rice, he forgot all about his pain and approached his brother's wife.

"Sister-in-law, please give just one bowl of rice to your younger brother-in-law."

p. 20

Immediately, the rice paddle came flying at Heungbu's cheek. It hit him so hard that his face burned as if his cheeks were on fire. He furtively raised his hands to his face and hurriedly stuffed the grains of rice that were stuck to his cheek into his mouth. Heungbu asked his sister-in-law to hit his other cheek with a rice paddle that had many grains of rice stuck to it. As soon as Nolbu's wife heard this request, she put down the rice paddle and beat Heungbu to her heart's content with the poker used to stoke the kitchen fire. Heungbu, whose body hurt so much that he could not even cry out in pain, dragged his aching body and barely managed to escape from Nolbu's house.

3
Heungbu Tries to Earn Money by Being Beaten

p.21

When it started getting late and Heungbu did not come home after going to get something to eat, Heungbu's wife grew worried. As she went outside the village to meet him, Heungbu staggered as he walked as if he were drunk. Heungbu's wife was glad to see him and ran to greet him. When she looked at him from far away, she didn't see anything to eat anywhere on Heungbu's body. But when she looked at him up close, she saw that blood was streaming from her husband's forehead and his eyes and cheeks were extremely swollen. Heungbu's wife, shocked to see her husband like this, asked him.

"Oh my, why is your face like that? Did your brother beat you?"

No matter how much his older brother had hurt his feelings, Heungbu could not bring himself to speak negatively of his brother.

"I got some rice and barley from my brother,

but my goodness, I came across some terrible thieves on the mountain road. Those thieves stole my grain and I ended up like this after fighting with them to try to stop them from stealing the money my brother gave me."

p.22

Heungbu's wife knew that he was lying, and she sank to the ground and cried bitterly. After observing Nolbu's behavior for so long, she could guess what had happened. Seeing her kind husband Heungbu speak well of his brother even after he had suffered only broke her heart even more.

Heungbu soothed his wife and his wife comforted him. After going through this, Heungbu's wife did any kind of work as soon as it came in.

Threshing grain, fetching water at dawn, making food for feasts at others' houses, washing the dishes after ancestral rites at others' houses…

Heungbu worked hard, just like his wife.

Shoveling feces at other people's houses, doing farm work in the middle of winter, fixing the roofs of houses in the neighborhood — he did all kinds of difficult work. But no matter how hard he worked, it was difficult for his family to get by.

One day, Heungbu secretly went to the government office to borrow some grain without his wife knowing. But he was told that the office did not lend out grain to people who did not even own any land, so Heungbu left in great disappointment. At that moment, the government office employee spoke carefully.

"By any chance, have you ever been flogged before?"

p.23

The employee said that a rich, elderly man in the neighboring village named Mr. Kim committed a crime and he was supposed to be beaten 30 times as punishment. However, he was sick at the moment, so he was trying to send someone else in his place.

When Heungbu heard that the person who took the beating in Mr. Kim's place would be paid 30 nyang, he said he would do it. He did this because when he closed his eyes tight, he thought about his entire family being able to eat until they were full. The government office employee gave him 5 nyang for the time being and told him to come to the office tomorrow morning.

In front of his house, Heungbu called his wife in a loud voice. Heungbu placed the 5 nyang in his wife's hand and told her what had happened. Heungbu's wife listened to her husband explain that he would earn money by being beaten and she began to cry.

"How could we eat rice that was bought with money that you earned by being beaten? If you die after being beaten, how will I and our young children live? Please, for heaven's sake, return that money and act as if nothing ever happened."

p.24

Heungbu reassured his crying wife, and the following day, he ran to the government office early in the morning.

"My name is Heungbu. I'm here to receive the beating instead of the elderly Mr. Kim."

A government office employee came and brought Heungbu to the place where he would be beaten.

When Heungbu lay down and was preparing to be beaten, a person came and spoke in a loud voice.

"Something good has happened in our country. I bring you the news that all criminals who have not killed a person are to be released. As such, go on and hurry back to your home."

What kind of bolt out of the blue was this?

Tears streamed down Heungbu's face as he pitied himself for having to go home empty-handed. While he walked up the mountain road to his house, his wife came running to meet him. She knew that her husband had gone to be beaten, so at dawn she had gone to draw water from the well and wish that Heungbu would return safely. When she saw Heungbu return safely, Heungbu's wife could not conceal her joy. Seeing his wife like that only made Heungbu's heart ache even more.

The next day, the son of elderly Mr. Kim came to find Heungbu and thank him for being willing to take the beating even though he did not end up getting beaten, and gave him some money. Heungbu tried not to take the money, but the man secretly slipped him the money and left, so Heungbu couldn't give it back. When he saw his wife beaming, Heungbu also smiled broadly for the first time in a long while.

4
Heungbu Saves a Swallow

p.26

The weather was gradually getting warmer, and soon it was March. The swallows that had flown south returned and began building a nest under the eaves of Heungbu's house. The children were happy to see the swallows, but Heungbu and his wife felt sorry for the swallows building their nest in a place that was not sturdy. Meanwhile, a pair of swallows quickly built a nest and laid eggs in it. Some time later, beautiful baby swallows hatched from the eggs. The swallow couple worked hard to find food and bring it back for their babies, and the baby swallows were busy being fed.

One day, while the swallow couple was away from their nest, a large serpent made its way up to the nest. One of Heungbu's children saw it and screamed in shock. Heungbu came running with a tree branch in his hands, but all of the baby swallows had become the serpent's food, and there was only one baby swallow left.

p.27

At the moment the serpent tried to catch and eat the last baby swallow, the baby swallow shakily flew up into the air, then fell to the ground.

Heungbu cradled the baby swallow and took a careful look at it. The baby swallow's right leg was broken.

"Dear, this swallow's leg is broken. We'd better hurry and treat the broken leg."

Heungbu devotedly took care of the swallow. The young swallow got better bit by bit, and after one week had passed, it began to fly. The swallow couple taught their baby how to catch food and how to fly in the sky. In the meantime, summer passed and autumn arrived.

"Now it's time for you all to leave and go somewhere warm in the south. Be safe on your long journey. The eaves of our house will be empty, so make sure to come back again next spring."

The swallow family left Heungbu's family's house and returned to the warm swallow kingdom. The ruler of the swallow kingdom discovered the swallow whose leg had been injured and asked what had happened. The baby swallow explained what had happened at Heungbu's family's house in detail.

"We should reward the sincerity of someone who regarded a swallow's life as precious and took care of it. How should we repay this kindness?"

p.28

"Yes, please let Heungbu escape from poverty and live in comfort."

The ruler of the swallow kingdom gave a small gourd seed to the swallow. The swallow wanted to give the seed to Heungbu quickly, so it eagerly waited for spring to come.

Finally, spring arrived. The swallow carried the gourd seed in its mouth and flew a long ways back to Heungbu's family's house. Heungbu, who was sweeping the yard, recognized the swallow and shouted in surprise.

"The swallow came back. The swallow with the injured leg came back."

Heungbu was as happy as if his own child had come back home, so he danced around joyfully. The swallow dropped the seed from its mouth in front of Heungbu. Heungbu planted the seed that he got from the swallow beneath the roof.

5

Heungbu's Family Cuts Open the Gourds

p.29

Only one day after the seed was planted, four gourds each as large as a full moon grew on the underneath Heungbu's family's roof. Even the villagers who saw the gourds as they passed by were shocked by their size.

In no time at all, it was almost Chuseok. The smell of food from other people's houses pierced their noses, but Heungbu's family did not even have enough rice to boil one bowl of porridge.

The whole family gathered in the yard after deciding to cut up a gourd and boil it into soup. Heungbu and his wife sat across from each other and began to saw.

"Easy, easy! Hurry and cut it open!"

When Heungbu pushed, his wife pulled, and they shouted together as they cut the gourd, so they had fun and cheered up.

Suddenly, the gourd split open with a crack, and a boy came out from inside of the gourd. The boy held out his arms full of colorful bottles and medicinal herbs as he said:

p.30

"This is medicine to bring a dead person back to life, and this is medicine that stops you from aging. Here are hundreds of medicines to cure any disease and directions for how to use them, so use them well."

As soon as he finished speaking, the boy disappeared.

Heungbu and his wife were completely out of their minds as if they were possessed by a ghost. The children who were next to them insisted that they should cut open the second gourd, so Heungbu and his wife began to cut the gourd again.

"Pop!"

Splendid treasures came pouring out from the second gourd. There were also two boxes made out of wood. Heungbu was curious, so he slightly opened one and looked inside. One was full of rice and the other was full of money.

Heungbu and his wife were overjoyed. They cooked the rice in an iron pot and they used the money to buy meat and boil some soup. They ate until they were full; they were so full that it felt like their stomachs would explode.

After they ate, Heungbu's son opened the box that had held the rice. When he looked inside, he was shocked. The box was full of rice again! Heungbu opened the box that had held the money and looked inside; that box was also full of money again. Even if they kept taking rice and money out of them, the boxes kept filling back up.

p.32

"Father, I want to buy a wonderful house this time."

At his children's words, Heungbu began cutting another gourd once again.

Just as the children had wished, dozens of people came out of the third gourd and began to build a house. In the blink of an eye, an enormous house suddenly appeared. There were a large garden full of grain, horses, cows, and everything they could think of.

Heungbu joyfully spoke to his wife, whose mouth was gaping open in shock.

"My dear, let's try cutting open the last gourd."

The people who came out of the last guard started doing housework. Heungbu's family had always spent their lives working day and night for others, so they went inside the room, not knowing what to do. Inside, a table was set full of food and there were even silk clothes and blankets prepared for them.

"It looks like we've received this good fortune because you've been such a kind person all your life."

Hearing the words of his wife, who had suffered with him all those years, Heungbu held her hand.

From that day on, Heungbu's family wore

silk clothes, ate until they were full, and lived happily with no need to do any hard work in their nice house.

6
Nolbu Visits Heungbu's House

p.33

Rumors that Heungbu had become a wealthy man reached Nolbu's ears.

"They say that he has more than 100 people working for him, his cellars are packed full of grain, and that every room in his house is overflowing with jewels."

The servant was so excited to hear that the kind Heungbu had become rich that saliva flew from his mouth as he spoke. But no matter how he thought about it, Nolbu could not believe those rumors.

"Heungbu even gave away his own food when he met a pitiful person. It would be difficult for him to save money and become wealthy. So then, did he gather up some assets by stealing? Or did he pick up a goblin's bat or something? No, it must be a false rumor."

Nolbu shook his head as he went here and there. But Nolbu's wife also heard the rumors, and she could not stand it.

p.34

"Oh, goodness, my stomach, my stomach hurts so much that I can't go on. Dear, hurry and go find out whether the rumors are true or not."

Nolbu went around asking which neighborhood Heungbu lived in. Finally, he arrived at Heungbu's house and just seeing its exterior made his jaw drop. Would even the house of a king be better than this?

"Heungbu, you scoundrel!"

Nolbu shouted with all his might. Heungbu and his wife came running out to greet Nolbu in their socks.

"Welcome, my brother!"

"Brother-in-law, have you been well?"

Nolbu did not even receive their greetings and screamed at them.

"Heungbu, you crook, just how much did you steal in order to become this wealthy?"

Heungbu did not know what was going on, but he made an effort to calm down his brother. Nolbu wanted to quickly hear how Heungbu had become rich, but he couldn't ask him directly to his face, so he kept grumbling for no reason.

"If the ancestors blessed you with fortune and made you wealthy, you should have come to see me. How could you just stop visiting me like this?"

p.35

"I wanted to go and see you again, but you told me to never appear before your eyes again, so I was hesitating."

Nolbu asked Heungbu again how he had become wealthy and Heungbu told him everything that had happened since the previous spring in detail. After hearing Heungbu's story, Nolbu cheered to himself on the inside.

Nolbu stood up in a hurry, and then his eyes fell on the closet that was placed on the floor. At a glance, it looked like quite a valuable item.

"That looks really nice. I wish you would give it to me as a gift."

"Alright, then I'll tell my servants to bring it over to your house."

Nolbu was worried that the closet would break when the servants moved it, so he struggled to bring it to his house all by himself.

p.36

As he arrived and went to put down the closet, he told his wife about the story he had heard from Heungbu. As soon as Nolbu finished talking, Nolbu's wife began to roll around on the floor.

"Oh my, so the rumors that Heungbu suddenly struck it rich were true! Goodness, my stomach hurts so much that I think I might die."

Nolbu spoke to his wife in a small voice.

"Dear, I have a good plan. Let's go and catch a swallow for ourselves!"

Upon hearing those words, a smile filled Nolbu's wife's face. She threw open the door and shouted.

"Hahaha! Hey, swallows, fly on over to our house."

7
Nolbu Goes to Catch a Swallow

p.37

After that day, Nolbu and his wife eagerly waited for spring to arrive. Finally, it was spring. A pair of swallows, which they had long been waiting for, built a nest under the eaves of Nolbu's house. Nolbu and his wife danced with joy as if they had already obtained a gourd seed with treasure coming out of it. From that time on, Nolbu and his wife were so afraid that someone would come and steal it that they sat underneath their roof and protected the swallow's nest.

Thankfully, the swallows laid five eggs under Nolbu's roof. Nolbu was so happy that he climbed up a ladder and touched the swallow's eggs every day. But Nolbu touched them so much that most of the eggs turned rotten or broke, and there was only one egg left. From the one remaining egg, a baby swallow awakened.

"Now all I have to do is breaking that swallow's leg!"

But this, too, was as difficult and wearisome as waiting for the swallows had been. So,

Nolbu ordered his servants to catch a large serpent and bring it back. And then, Nolbu put that serpent near the swallows' nest.

p.38

"The serpent has to attack the swallows' nest so the baby swallow will fall out of the nest with shock and break its leg."

That's what Nolbu thought as he drove the serpent toward the swallows' nest with a stick. Nolbu kept hitting the serpent's head with the stick, so the serpent attacked Nolbu. After running away in shock, Nolbu thought of a good plan. He climbed the ladder up to the swallows' nest, and in the blink of an eye — "snap" — he broke the sleeping swallow's leg. Then, he loudly cried with sadness.

"Goodness, this poor little thing. The swallow broke its leg trying to run away from the nasty serpent. Boohoo!"

p.39

Upon hearing the sound of the swallow's leg breaking, Nolbu's wife woke up from a nap and began to hum a song. As she treated the swallow's leg, she said.

"What a happy occasion!"

The swallow cried as it flew south, and it told the ruler of the swallows the truth. Once again, the ruler of the swallows gave a gourd seed to the swallow. When it became spring again, as soon as the swallow came back to Nolbu's house with the seed in its mouth, Nolbu and his wife were so excited that they didn't know what to do.

"So you finally came back, swallow. We fixed your broken leg last year, so if you haven't forgotten our kindness, give us that gourd seed."

The swallow dropped the seed from its mouth into the palms of their hands. Nolbu immediately planted the seed in a place that received a lot of sunlight. Not long afterward, the seeds rapidly grew and sprouted into ten large gourds.

"That scoundrel Heungbu became rich with only four gourds, so how rich will I be with ten gourds? How will I ever use all that money?"

Nolbu was so excited by the thought of becoming rich that he danced with joy.

8

Nolbu's Family Cuts Open the Gourds

p.40

Finally, Nolbu began to cut open one of the large gourds.

"Easy, easy! Easy does it! Gold and silver, clothes made out of silk, all that treasure, come on out!"

But no matter how much he sawed, the gourd was as hard as a rock, so he could not cut it open. It was the same even when he called a servant to saw it. So, he called a strong worker to cut it open.

Crack! With a sound like thunder, the gourd finally split open. But the treasure Nolbu had called for did not come out. Instead, an old man came out, stroking his beard as he walked. He immediately shouted at Nolbu.

"Hey, Nolbu, you scoundrel, when are you going to repay the three thousand nyang that your grandfather's grandfather borrowed from me?"

Nolbu snorted at the old man's words. There was no way Nolbu would just pay back a debt to some ancestor whose name he didn't even know.

p.41

"Kids, hurry and come teach this crook Nolbu a lesson!"

As soon as the old man finished speaking, people came rushing out of the gourd and tied Nolbu up in a tree. He could only come down after he paid the three thousand nyang.

Nolbu was so upset about his money being taken away that he couldn't even breathe. But he comforted himself with the thought that there were still many gourds left, and he cut open another gourd.

Crack! As soon as the second gourd split open, the sound of a moktak rang out as a monk appeared.

"Nolbu, you scoundrel, we prayed and prayed for your sake to Buddha, but seeing how you are still empty-handed, this cannot go on any longer."

Upon hearing these words, Nolbu hurried into his house, took out one thousand nyang, and gave it to the monk. The monk said that he had to have five thousand nyang, so Nolbu put more and more money into the monk's gourd. But strangely, as soon as the money went into the gourd, it disappeared without a trace.

Nolbu was very angry, but he decided to try cutting open the third gourd. This time, beggars came out of the gourd and merrily danced in the yard as if it were their own house.

"We purposely came here after hearing that Nolbu is a generous person. Let's play to our hearts' content."

p.42

They made a big fuss as they demanded rice, alcohol, and money. Nolbu was worried that the beggars would take away all his possessions, so he gave them money and rice and chased them away. Believing that there would really be treasure inside this time, he cut open the gourds one by one, but only dreadful things kept happening.

Crack! The people who came out of the ninth gourd were carrying hammers and axes, and they violently beat Nolbu and his wife. Looking at them closely, these people couldn't see or had something wrong with their bodies. They were all people who had suffered because of Nolbu. He barely managed to calm them down, but nevertheless, they took everything he had, even the deeds to his land.

p.43

Worried that something even more terrible might happen, the workers all ran away. Nolbu and his wife were so upset about the money they had lost that they pounded the ground and cried. Now they were afraid to cut open the last remaining gourd.

Still, Nolbu could not throw away the expectation that somehow treasure might come out of that gourd.

"We have nothing left to give now, so since we have nothing to lose, let's cut it open."

The two of them combined their strength and cut open the last gourd.

"Easy, easy. It doesn't matter if it's silver or gold, as long as a lot of it comes out."

The gourd split open bit by bit, and a yellow light shone from the inside. This time, it really seemed like gold. A slightly strange smell came out, but as soon as they saw the yellow light, they automatically cheered up.

With a loud "crack!," yellow waste water came gushing out of the gourd and filled the entire house.

"Goodness, someone save me!"

Nolbu fell into the waste water and screamed for someone to save him, but no one helped him. Nolbu and his wife barely managed to swim out and escape.

Completely covered in feces, Nolbu and his wife, who had lost their house, their money, and everything they had in the blink of an eye, walked toward Heungbu's house.

9

Close Brothers

p.45

At the sight of his brother in such an appalling state, Heungbu came rushing outside.

"Brother, my brother, what happened? Let's hurry inside."

Heungbu brought Nolbu, Nolbu's wife, and their children into the house.

"Brother, don't worry about anything and rest comfortably."

Heungbu hurried to put his brother and his brother's wife in the master bedroom of the house, then gave them something to eat and something to wear as he comforted them. Some time later, he found a good place and built a house as large and nice as his own for them. In addition, he prepared household items, clothes, and food that were the same as his own for them.

"Heungbu, thank you so much!"

Although Nolbu had been a terrible scoundrel, he was touched by Heungbu's kind heart and reflected on his past mistakes, and the brothers got along well with each other.

After that, Heungbu lived a long and happy life, and all of his descendants were healthy and enjoyed wealth. It was said that everyone in the world praised the virtue of Heungbu, and his name remained in their memories for a long, long time.

MEMO

MEMO

MEMO

Darakwon Korean Readers

흥부전 The Story of Heungbu

Adapted by Kim Yu Mi, Bae Se Eun
Translated by Katelyn Hemmeke
First Published October, 2020
Publisher Chung Kyudo
Editor Lee Suk-hee, Baek Da-heuin, Park Inkyung
Cover Design Yoon Ji-young
Interior Design Yoon Hyun-ju
Illustrator SOUDAA
Voice Actor Shin So-yun, Kim Rae-whan

Published by Darakwon Inc.
Darakwon Bldg., 211 Munbal-ro, Paju-si, Gyeonggi-do
Republic of Korea 10881
Tel : 02-736-2031 Fax : 02-732-2037
(Marketing Dept. ext.: 250~252, Editorial Dept. ext.: 420~426)

Price 9,000 won

ISBN 978-89-277-3262-4 14710
978-89-277-3259-4 (set)

Visit the Darakwon homepage to learn about our other
publications and promotions and to download the contents of
the MP3 format.

http://www.darakwon.co.kr
http://koreanbooks.darakwon.co.kr